INTERNAL ACHIEVEMENT

WALTER LEIGH BATES

INTERNAL ACHIEVEMENT

Copyright © 2007 by Walter Leigh Bates

ISBN: 0-9770398-5-4
978-0-9770398-5-2

Published by

LifeBridge
BOOKS
P.O. BOX 49428
CHARLOTTE, NC 28277

Printed in the United States of America.

DEDICATION

*To the closest person on earth to me, my darling
wife of 30 years, Delores ("Baby Girl"), who has stood
faithfully by my side and watched with me as God has
exercised His faithfulness in our ministry and personal lives.
Together we have cried, laughed, prayed and believed Him
all the way from where we were to where we are today.
Thank God for helping us to remain committed to
Him and to each other till death do us part.*

*To my three daughters Adrienne (Nathaniel) Green,
Michelle (Edward) Cook and Sonia (Mario) Brown—
my only biological child in the world. To my Executive
Assistant, Gwen Anderson (my God-daughter), who has
untiringly worked by my side to help put together this
manuscript; to Phyllis Malone, my Executive Administrative
Assistant and my awesome staff: Shirley Smith (my sister) and
Youth Pastor Sherral Dulaney. To my church family, Balm
in Gilead for All People Worship Center, to all my
sons and daughters in the Lord, to my mother, aunts,
uncle, brother and sisters and my God-parents,
Evangelist Maria (DT) Gardner Thomas.*

CONTENTS

FOREWORD

One of the greatest challenges we have as people is to remain focused until goals and achievements are accomplished. There are so many things around which distract us until we lose the desire to gain what it was that we started with.

In the book *Internal Achievement*, Dr. Walter Leigh Bates has taken the complexity of distraction and given us instruction on how to first accomplish on the inside the goals that we've set to experience and enjoy on the outside. As you read this book, I am convinced it will give you information and insight that will help you achieve any God-given goal. If you can see it in your heart, this book will show you how to have it in your hand. I encourage you to read these pages and be blessed."

– Bishop Darrell L. Hines
Senior Pastor/Founder
Christian Faith Fellowship Church
Milwaukee, Wisconsin

INTRODUCTION

Looking from the outside in, and getting the opportunity to examine all the things going on in the minds of other successful people, would be an ideal situation to be in: take notes, repeat their mental patterns, copy the same traits and tendencies and get the same results. Sounds real easy doesn't it? Sorry, this will never happen. But there is a way to become informed without following others. I can assure you that achievement is not reached by going to a physical place, wearing certain clothes, knowing specific people, attending a special college, living in a major suburb or following the crowd. Money can't buy success and references are not necessary.

This book is structured by the leading of our Lord the All-Knowing Omniscient One. It is designed to inform and target those areas in our lives that, if given the right attention and with much needed effort put forth, will cause consistent patterns to be established and continue to be accomplished. This inward activity will affect your outside results.

Make it a lifestyle—not a 30, 60, or 90-day project where you stop and celebrate. Do it every year, every month, every week, every day, hour, minute and second—and don't procrastinate.

Let these words motivate you to experience your personal

"Internal Achievement" in every area of your existence: spiritual, physical, mental, verbal, audible, financial, educational and social. Each needs special targeted efforts.

It is my prayer that every chapter of this book will define and encourage your "inward" spiritual interactions and you will achieve the destiny God has planned especially for you.

— Walter Leigh Bates

CHAPTER I

THE INVISIBLE DECISION

The greatest exercises ever performed are not practiced in a gym using free weights, walking on treadmills, flexing in front of a mirror or targeting major body groups.

While this may be extremely rewarding when you see the final results days, weeks or months later, the most effective activity is what takes place on the inside. What you envision internally motivates and fuels your work.

In this book, when we talk of *internal* achievement it includes what occurs in both the mind and heart—and how it affects us psychologically, emotionally and spiritually. And by *achievement* we are focusing on action, performance and production.

GOD'S PATTERN OF SUCCESS

I believe personal achievement comes in three stages: (1) you mentally desire something, (2) you work to attain it and (3) you finally hold it in your hands.

This is the biblical pattern of success. Immediately after Moses died and Joshua became the leader of the children of Israel, God told him, *"This book of the law shall not depart out of thy mouth; but thou shalt meditate therein day and night, that thou mayest observe to do according to all that is written therein: for then thou shalt make thy way prosperous, and then thou shalt have good success"* (Joshua 1:8).

This divine directive is also intended for you and me today. Instead of God's Word entering and then leaving you, the scriptures are to remain inward—not to *"depart."*

According to God's order, it all begins in the mind; you *"meditate."* Second, you *"observe to do"*—or take action. As a direct result your way will be made *"prosperous"* and you will *"have good success."*

The Lord encouraged Joshua to *exercise* the word of God *invisibly* within himself. The Almighty gave him this charge, not only so he would possess these virtues, but that his actions would be an example to the children of Israel—causing them to seek their promised inheritance.

INVISIBLE ROADS

As you continue reading, you will discover internal achievement precedes external possession.

The roads which lead us to physical, tangible, physiological, even monetary results, are invisible. Even though the finish line may be crossed in plain view, the real race is run on the inside.

12

---- 💜 ----

*Internal achievers must ward off the temptation
to watch and worry over what other people are doing—
what they possess, how much education they
have received, their social status, physical
appearance or even their spiritual walk.*

The internal race has no competitors, no spectators and receives no standing ovation or applause.

The hurdles you will encounter on your road to victory lie deep within you: fear, doubt, suspicion, apprehension, procrastination, inferiority complexes, low self esteem and poor self image. Later in this book, you will see how these can be conquered.

A TIME OF REFLECTION

When God instructed Joshua to *meditate* on the Word night and day, the Hebrew term for this is *ha ga,* which means the act of reflection, thoughtful deliberation and careful consideration. Simply stated, don't be in a big hurry for action!

I was surprised when I learned the word *meditate* also refers to the cow, which has two stomach compartments, one to digest a meal and the other to store enough for a later period of time. The animal then chews what is called cud, the portion of food which returns from the first stomach to the mouth to be chewed a second time. In the process, the cow ponders or ruminates on his food supply. Bison, buffalo, deer, antelopes, giraffes and camels all chew cud.

THE FOLLY OF EXTERNAL ANSWERS

What is the great desire and longing of your heart? What are you meditating on pertaining to your future?

Often, we hear the exact solution to our needs through a message, a verse of scripture or a testimony that targets how God's promises can be fulfilled. However, in our limited view, we are often prone to only *observe* the answer and treat it as peripheral—external to our situation. So instead of seeking God's presence, having access to His wisdom and praying for a revelation which will show us His will, we become carnal, looking for the answers in human experience.

As a result, we wind up in a condition described by the apostle Paul: *"Now the works* [deeds, actions] *of the flesh* [carnal man] *are manifest, which are these; adultery, fornication, uncleanness, lasciviousness, idolatry, witchcraft, hatred, variance* [disagreeing, discords], *emulations* [opposition, antagonism, rivalry], *wrath, strife"* (Galatians 5:19-20).

These are all "outside" influences which leave us unfulfilled and dissatisfied.

"Inside" success is found in the words of Jesus when He says, *"...for, behold, the kingdom of God is within you"* (Luke 17:21).

GET READY!

Regardless of what you pursue, whether academics, physical health, finances or your spiritual life, the journey begins with an invisible decision. Yet, what you embrace on the inside determines what will eventually be demonstrated in *all* areas of life.

The internal tunnel may be dark and filled with detours, but one day soon your path will break into the sunlight. All the time of quiet, thoughtful, prayerful preparation will suddenly blossom like a flower after the cold of winter.

Get ready! God is preparing you for achievement beyond anything you can ask or think.

CHAPTER 2

RIGHT THINGS IN— WRONG THINGS OUT

O ur personal accomplishments are the result of motive or incentive. When these two factors are applied, our "inner urges" cause us to:

- Behave and react in a certain way.
- Visualize ourselves in a specific situation.
- Reach toward a desired objective.
- Seize an opportunity.
- Overcome an obstacle.
- Endure a challenge.

In addition, these "inner urges" protect us by warning what *not* to respond to. They become a cautionary signal which helps us avoid the wrong motives and influences.

A BROKEN-HEARTED ARMY

The important principle of choosing right over wrong is demonstrated in the life of David.

After he returned from battle, he found his hometown of Ziklag had been burned to the ground and all the women and children had been taken prisoner.

———————❤———————

Surveying the situation outwardly caused David's army to cry until they had no more tears to shed. The men were broken-hearted, depressed and so overwhelmed and distraught over the loss of their families they thought of stoning their leader.

David, too, was extremely distressed, but he had to rise above the dire circumstances, exchanging his *wrong* outlook for the *right* thoughts and feelings.

DAVID'S SOURCE OF STRENGTH

How did David fight off the negative emotions which were trying to smother his confidence? He found a place of solitude, began to pray and strengthened himself with trust in Almighty God.

David inquired of the Lord, *"Shall I pursue after this troop? shall I overtake them? And he answered him, Pursue:*

for thou shalt surely overtake them, and without fail recover all" (1 Samuel 30:8).

With his army of 600 and God's directive, David began the pursuit of the Amalekites. But at the brook called Besor, 200 of the men were so fatigued, exhausted they dropped out of the battle.

Discovering the location of the raiders, David's army pounced on them and *"...recovered all that the Amalekites had carried away...And there was nothing lacking to them, neither small nor great, neither sons nor daughters, neither spoil, nor any thing that they had taken to them: David recovered all. And David took all the flocks and the herds, which they drave before those other cattle, and said, This is David's spoil"* (vv.18-20).

AN INWARD PURGING

There is a place of communion with God where He meets us and gives us the desire to move forward. It is here we receive our heavenly instructions.

Before David's external victory, he experienced an internal achievement. This happened when he took the right things in—and forced the wrong things out. He asked God to purge him of uncertainty, doubt and hesitation. These weaknesses were replaced with a spirit of pursuing, advancing and overcoming obstacles.

In the midst of conflict, only our Heavenly Father can equip our hearts and minds with the correct thoughts, desires and motives. Even more, the Lord will arm us with tactics and strategies to overcome the enemy.

As a direct result of an inward transformation, David was able to defeat the Amalekites, declare "success" and recover all the spoils.

"SHARE AND SHARE ALIKE"

Communication with God will give us an inward vision which shows us moving forward. The Lord *reveals* progress to us even before He gives the order to advance. Plus, He tells us how to handle victory.

When David returned to Brook Besor, he informed the 200 men who were too weak to fight of the great victory. However, the soldiers who courageously fought the battle said, "Since these men didn't help in the rescue, they have no right to the plunder we recovered."

David disagreed, telling them, "Don't be selfish. You can't operate this way." He informed them that the share of one who stayed behind is equal to the person who fights" (v.24). In other words, "Share and share alike!"

FIND YOUR CLOSET!

Inner success is achieved by following what Jesus says in the Sermon on the Mount. He declares, *"But thou, when thou prayest, enter into thy closet* [hidden, away from others]*, and* *when thou hast shut thy door, pray to thy Father* [the Source] *which is in secret; and thy Father which seeth in secret shall reward thee openly* [visibly]*"* (Matthew 6:6).

Jesus is not speaking of a physical closet in your house. Rather, He is referring to the invisible, secluded place within ourselves.

———————— ♥ ————————

As David experienced long ago, our achievement springs from the inner ability God created in us. We use His gift of transformation—exchanging what is on the inside and duplicating it on the outside.

Every image of success is given to us from the Father. As we study and embrace what He shows us in His Word, He strengthens, inspires and motivates us. As He speaks by His Spirit, we discern what to welcome and what to discard. This is how we allow the right things to enter and determine what should be thrown away!

Like a mountain climber, we stand on the summit in our heart and mind long before we reach the peak with our feet.

CHAPTER 3

WHAT GOOD IS CHRIST AND RELIGION?

The title of this chapter is a question which was frequently asked by believers and non-Christians alike when, in 1987, several renowned television evangelists were displayed by the media as complete failures in the world of Christendom. It was a devastating blow and black-eye to the faith of multitudes in many denominations.

Hearts were broken, the leadership of the church was severely damaged and faith appeared to be shattered. From the world's view, the Church had lost its glory. Many supporters who were affected voiced their opinions through lawsuits. After all, they were the people who helped build those ministries.

It was at this point in prayer that God revealed to me "a rhema Word" for the situation." He asked, "Walter, what good is Christ and religion?" Then He proceeded to tell me how the eyes of the saints on earth must be refocused on the *real* reason for Christ, the Church, religion and salvation.

This headline-making event also demonstrated the great difference between *external,* worldly-based judgment and *internal,* spiritually-based achievement.

THE REAL ISSUE

While men may appear to be flawless through the eyes of those using only their five senses, we the Church—those who have experienced a real manifestation of salvation—must center on the true issue, which is Christ, the Provider of Salvation for the World.

The Bible tells us, *"But as many as received him, to them gave he power to become the sons of God, even to them that believe on his name: Which were born, not of blood, nor of the will of the flesh, nor of the will of man, but of God"* (John 1:12-13).

Later, the apostle Paul explains the *process* of salvation. He writes, *"But God commendeth his love toward us, in that, while we were yet sinners, Christ died for us. Much more then, being now justified by his blood, we shall be saved from wrath through him. For if, when we were enemies, we were reconciled to God by the death of his Son, much more, being reconciled, we shall be saved by his life. And not only so, but we also joy in God through our Lord Jesus Christ, by whom we have now received the atonement"* (Romans 5:8-11).

What a marvelous gift!

REQUIREMENTS FOR TRANSFORMATION

As you read scripture there is an underlying concept which describes unregenerated man. It is called "depravity." Interpreted, this means mankind is born unrighteous and in an unregenerated state—a transgressor of God's divine law. He cannot live or experience righteousness on his own, and in this sinful state he cannot turn from or change.

Man needs to see and recognize his destructive nature, because it leaves him totally disconnected from his Creator and Maker, who is God.

Three things are required for us to be miraculously changed from the inside out:

- First: Through Jesus Christ man is led to see himself as a sinner in rebellion against God.
- Second: He is able to understand and have proof of the sacrifice and righteousness of the Savior who can save him from sin.
- Third: He needs to be reminded that if he refuses to receive the Savior, he will face a certain judgment without hope of anything but condemnation.

As John tells us, when we receive Christ, something extraordinary takes place. We are given *by Christ*—not by man—the *"power to become the sons of God"* (John 1:12).

A miraculous transformation occurs. Internally, our position is changed from one level to another—from a *lower* state before receiving Christ to a *higher* position as a son of the Most High God.

First, however, we must receive permission—or *admission*—by one who has a right to grant it by authority. This is delegated to Christ by the Father to receive you into a godly state of Sonship

"SONS AND HEIRS"

The apostle Paul uses the example of the Jewish tutoring of sons to help make clear to us what takes place. He writes to the believers of Galatia, *"Now I say, that the heir, as long as he is a child, differeth nothing from a servant, though he be Lord of all; But is under tutors and governors until the time appointed of the father. Even so we, when we were children, were in bondage under the elements of the world: but when the fullness of the time was come, God sent forth his son, made of a woman, made under the law, to redeem them that were under the law, that we might receive the adoption of sons. And because ye are sons, God hath sent forth the Spirit of his Son into your hearts, crying Abba, Father. Wherefore thou are no more a servant, but a son; and if a son, then an heir of God through Christ"* (Galatians 4:1-7).

The Jewish son, until age 13, sat under people who were able to train and teach the child that he was an heir—a receiver of a great inheritance (the operations, expectations, responsibilities and desires of his father). There was an appointed time given by the father to instruct and prepare the child for his coming inheritance.

Likewise, in the process of accepting God's Son, the Father uses men as vessels to teach and make clear *Christ* to His people.

REDEEMED! REDEEMED!

Scripture tells us, *"The word is nigh thee, even in thy mouth, and in thy heart: that is, the word of faith, which we preach"* (Romans 10:8). So God appoints men in the earth realm to explain the Gospel (the Good News) as the plan of redemption and the answer for the sins of mankind.

Here is the message preached by Paul: *"That if thou shalt confess with thy mouth the Lord Jesus, and shalt believe in thine heart that God hath raised him from the dead, thou shalt be saved. For with the heart man believeth unto righteousness; and with the mouth confession is made unto salvation"* (vv.9-10).

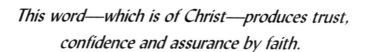

*This word—which is of Christ—produces trust,
confidence and assurance by faith.*

Clearly, faith is a *substance* to work with and, as it becomes alive in a person's mind, he begins to confess that Christ died and rose from the dead.

When these words are combined with faith, (which is trust in what is being revealed and made clear) they penetrate the heart and soul (the mind, the emotions). Then, like a steering wheel, they direct man's will (the decision channels). He asks for forgiveness and is united back together with God.

Once this happens, he is redeemed. Hallelujah!

We are "bought back"—freed from our captivity and bondage. Christ's blood, which was shed on Calvary, was the precious price paid to purchase us from sin and Satan's possession.

This message of Christ is taught through men, called apostles, prophets, pastors, evangelist and teachers (Ephesians 4:11). These specially appointed believers are able to continually enlighten us step by step as God reveals His truth through them.

LIBERTY AND BLESSINGS

When a child is young, in the position of a servant, he is subject to "orders" and restrictions and must respond by listening and doing what he is being told. This is comparable to people who have accepted Christ (which is an outward expression of spiritual devotion).

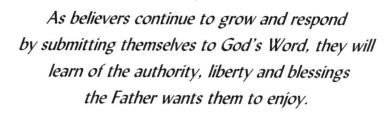

As believers continue to grow and respond
by submitting themselves to God's Word, they will
learn of the authority, liberty and blessings
the Father wants them to enjoy.

The Church and religion are only channels which bring people under the sound of the Gospel. This leads to salvation, which is *forgiveness* and pardon of the believer's sin (Acts 13:38; Ephesians 1:7; Colossians. 1:14). Remember, because of Adam's fall, all men are born in sin and can only be forgiven by God's sacrifice—His Son, Jesus Christ.

WE ARE JUSTIFIED

The *penalty* of sin is spiritual death, meaning to be cut off from God's presence for eternity and tormented in hell eternally.

Thank God, there is deliverance through Christ. By faith, we become partakers of His Holy Righteousness (Romans 4:11-12, 22; 2 Corinthians 5:19).

Then *regeneration* takes place, which means we are re-created or "born again" spiritually—"converted" and restored to a better, higher, more worthy state. We are also *justified*, or "declared right"—treated as righteous and worthy of salvation.

God justifies all who believe in the Lord Jesus and declares the repenting sinner as righteous. The righteousness of the Father is imputed to the one who receives Christ as his personal Savior.

"I Know Who I Am"

What good is Christ and religion? Let's go back to the instruction of children—who were treated as "full grown" at the age of 13. It was then the child found out who he was and what his responsibilities were. After being instructed, taught and properly prepared, on that day he says "Abba, Father" (Galatians 4:6), which means, "I belong. I know who I am and what I was created for."

Through Christ, the Father has given each of us the power to become a son of God and a member of His family. Instead of being "churchy," we are *sanctified*—set apart—free from sin and purified.

God calls men and women from the world to Himself for His own purposes (Romans 8:29; 15:16, 1 Corinthians 6:11; Hebrews 10:10).

———————♥———————

Sanctification is positional and progressive and must be constantly and continually happening.

Every prayer we utter, every service we attend and every message or scripture interpretation we accept through faith *reconciles* us. It restores our friendship with God and settles any differences which may exist. Then the Lord draws us closer and closer unto Himself and we are no longer estranged from the Father. Instead, we are bought back into the right relationship to Him through His Son's finished work on the cross (Romans 5:10, 2 Corinthians 5:18-20).

THE "FOOLISHNESS" OF PREACHING

It is through Christ we find salvation and are no longer disconnected. God gives us the assurance of our salvation and helps us trust His Word (1 John 5:13; John 10:28; Romans.8:35-39).

The apostle Paul wrote to the believers at Corinth, *"For the preaching of the cross is to them that perish foolishness; but unto us which are saved it is the power of God"* (1 Corinthians 1:18).

We must constantly remind ourselves it is God's Word which releases His *power* into our lives. After all, it *"...pleased God by the foolishness of preaching to save them that believe"* (v.21).

ANOTHER COMFORTER

Jesus tells us, *"Even the Spirit of truth; whom the world cannot receive, because it seeth him not, neither knoweth him: but ye know him; for he dwelleth with you and shall be in you"* (John 14:17).

He was speaking of the Holy Spirit when He said, *"And I will pray the Father and he shall give you another Comforter* [which in the Greek means "Allos"— another of the same kind], *that he may abide with you for ever"* (v.16).

Judas then asks, *"Lord, how is it that thou wilt manifest thyself unto us, and not unto the world?"* (v.22).

Jesus answered, saying, *"If a man love me, he will keep my words: and my Father will love him, and we will come unto him, and make our abode with him"* (John 14:23).

Through the Word of God (who is Christ), the Father and the Holy Spirit "supernaturally" are united in the life of the believer. Even though fallible man falls short in the eyes of the world, God reminds us it is His Son, His Word and His Spirit that is given to all, and will lift the wrath from our lives.

SUPERNATURAL POWER

Regardless of the trials we face as Christians, we must remember we are living and practicing a life that is not natural, but *supernatural*—spiritually pleasing to God.

What good is Christ and religion? Jesus gives us this promise: *"But ye shall receive power, after that the Holy Ghost is come upon you"* (Acts 1:8).

What is this power?

- *Exousia*—delegated influence.
- *Dunamis*—strength and miracle power.
- *Dunastes*—great authority.

32

Then God's Son declares, *"...and ye shall be witnesses unto me"* (v.8). This, in the Greek is *martus*—power to be willing to die for Him. It is a "stick-to-it" power, "hang on" power and "all the way in spite of yourself" power.

The disciples were persecuted and believers of the early church were placed in stadiums and made spectacles of for being Christians. Yet they were willing to die for Him and be His witnesses.

They spoke of His death, burial and resurrection and remained faithful because they believed the prophecy of Joel: *"...it shall come to pass...that I will pour out my spirit upon all flesh; and your sons and your daughters shall prophesy, your old men shall dream dreams, your young men shall see visions"* (Joel 2:28).

A WINNABLE FIGHT

You and I have tasted of that "heavenly gift." Through an internal miracle of a cleansed heart, we have been made partakers of the good Word of God. If we are tempted to fall away after so great a salvation, we must remind ourselves there is no other way to God. His Son came to earth, died and paid the price necessary for our salvation.

So when you feel weak, frustrated and ready to give up, remember the Word, which says, *"...the natural man receiveth not the things of the Spirit of God: for they are foolishness unto him: neither can he know them, because they are spiritually discerned...But we have the mind of Christ* (1 Corinthains 2:14,16).

Jesus promised He would be in us and with us at all times and one day, just as He said, He will return.

Hold tightly onto your faith; daily seeking God for a greater understanding.

- Our labor is not in vain.
- Our fight is winnable.
- Our work is workable.
- Our God is more than able.

The next time someone questions, "What good is Christ and religion?" tell them you serve a risen Savior—and without Him, we are forever lost.

CHAPTER 4

ORGANISMS OF CHRISTIANITY

I t's surprising how often we ask questions relating to food:

- "Have you had breakfast?"
- "Are you hungry?"
- "Did you eat anything today?"
- "How was your dinner?"

Survival, however, is not just food consumption, but a combination of vitamins, minerals and necessary nutrients being supplied to the body which are needed daily to effectively operate normal bodily functions. And just as the physical body needs to be constantly nourished to remain healthy, our spirit man must be ministered to every single day. For we are in a spiritual relationship that needs biblical and supernatural experiences and fellowship in order to function and progress—while at the same time fighting off our sworn enemy who we all know as the devil.

Maintaining our spiritual level is challenging and often appears difficult, but it can be achieved through proper knowledge and consistency.

OUR BASIC NEEDS

There are several "organic drives" or needs of every human being.

1. The need for comfort—the avoidance of pain and confusion.
2. The need of warmth when cold.
3. The need of cold when hot.
4. The need for water.
5. Clean air—when the air is polluted.
6. Sleep.
9. Protection when afraid.
8. Food.
9. Rest.

An organism—whether plant or animal—is a living, complete unit in and of itself. Everything God has made as a functioning living entity is created to survive on its own efforts. From the day of existence, the search for nourishment and survival begins.

Even though all the faculties of a newborn baby are not fully developed, the infant can smell the mother and it seeks for her. Once she is within reach, the baby is instinctively drawn to the mother's milk and will cry until placed where it can receive nourishment.

Likewise, every baptized, born again, Spirit-filled believer is responsible for receiving directions from the Lord into a place where spiritual growth and sustenance is plentiful and continually available.

---------♥---------

We are responsible for yielding to God's Word and becoming what the Creator desires for our lives.

"WHO IS LORD?"

If you want to know the source of every "good thing" and who we are to submit to, carefully read these words from scripture: *"And it came to pass, when Joshua was by Jericho, that he lifted up his eyes and looked, and, behold, there stood a man* [an angel in the likeness of human flesh] *over against him with his sword drawn in his hand: and Joshua went unto him, and said unto him, Art thou for us, or for our adversaries? And he said, Nay; but as captain of the host of the Lord am I now come. And Joshua fell on his face to the earth, and did worship, and said unto him, What saith my lord unto his servant? And the captain of the Lord's host said unto Joshua, Loose thy shoe from off thy foot; for the place whereon thou standest is holy. And*

37

Joshua did so" (Joshua 5:13-15).

Yes, Joshua was confronted by an angel—to whom he was directed to submit everything. This represents perhaps the greatest challenge to every believer—the test of authority and the answer to the question, "Who is Lord over your life?"

As we learn in the New Testament, Jesus Christ is Lord.

TOTAL SUBMISSION?

At first, Joshua was ready to confront the angel. In the passage above, the word "captain" in Hebrew is "sar" which means keeper, governor or ruler. And "sarar" means to "exercise dominion over."

There is only one conclusion we can make. As an "organism of Christianity"—which is the Christ life, or to be like Christ—we must first yield completely to Christ as Lord.

The angel also revealed to Joshua, *"the place whereon thou standest is holy."* It was God–filled, God-owned and God-controlled. And just as Joshua took off his shoes as a sign of humility and submission, we also are to surrender ourselves and give God control of all areas of our lives. There must be the element of reverence and sacredness available to God.

If you keep reading the book of Joshua (chapter 6) you'll find that Jericho is the next test of victory awaiting him.

BEYOND YOUR STRENGTH

Before the Almighty reveals what is available to the people

of God, full submission must be placed in the Lord's hands. It's the only way we can survive the huge challenges looming just around the corner.

The apostle Paul prays, *"And the very God of peace sanctify you wholly* [completely—body, soul, spirit/mind, will, emotions]; *and I pray God your whole spirit* [place of revelation and fellowship] *and soul and body* [place of bodily appetite and channel of five senses] *be preserved blameless unto the coming of our Lord Jesus Christ"* (1 Thessalonians 5:23).

Paul is disclosing three major areas of attack the devil specifically aims for to hinder growth and spiritual survival in the life of the Christian.

First, only God can bring satisfaction and wholeness to our lives. Second, there is a call for us to excel in this spiritual walk through yielding ourselves to God so He can do in us what we cannot do in our own strength. Third, the total person is to be set apart in mind, body, heart, spirit and soul, because our relationship with God involves our whole being—*all of us*.

———❤———

Through sanctification, God by His Spirit is setting us apart for His purpose so we can be Christ-like, progressing toward the goal of maturity and becoming like Jesus.

OUR CRAVINGS AND DESIRES

The major problem is the devil attacks our *soulish* nature

(the mind, will, and emotions) through thoughts and reasoning, which "pull at" and challenge us to make a decision through the will, which is the "choice" channel. Or, Satan uses his power to disturb our seat of emotions to influence feelings of doubt, depression, anxiety, frustration and impulsiveness to persuade us through natural feelings to make unwise, unspiritual decisions that stunt survival and growth of the Christ-like life.

Then he exerts pressure through the five senses (sight, taste, touch, smell and hearing) to allure the believer to respond to physical instead of spiritual matters.

Satan loves to tempt the body and its appetites, cravings and desires. So, unless these areas are totally surrendered to Christ as Lord through the Word of God, the *organism* (baptized believer) is impeded from continuing to survive in the spiritual relationship which is established through salvation. This makes *continuation* of *development* impossible, thus ending the godly experience and now inviting weakness and malnourishment.

OUR DIRECT ACCESS

The Bible tells us, *"But we all, with open face beholding as in a glass the glory of the Lord, are changed* [transformed] *into the same image from glory to glory, even as by the Spirit of the Lord"* (2 Corinthians 3:18).

Paul is explaining that the Word of God is constantly showing the believer a higher spiritual plane. And as the Word is read and received we see through *beholding* (fixed eyes, gazing—to go into a type of visualization, seeing what the Word is revealing). We place ourselves in union (becoming one with) and communion (fellowship) with the Word and *impartation* takes place.

In this glorious process, we begin to receive what we visualize and start departing from what we are, to become what we see (which is Christ). And as we keep our eyes focused on that image—seeking, desiring and aspiring to be like Him—the same Spirit which led the Lord will also lead us into perfection and true spiritual development and growth.

The open face of the Father is unveiled. There is no curtain, no earthly high priest who has to intercede to God on our behalf and first offer up sacrifices for sins, then receive forgiveness.

————————❤————————

We can go ourselves, on our own desire and submission, directly to God through His Word, and receive what we need to believe Jesus for.

God's glory, which is His presence sealed in His Word, takes us higher and higher in our standard of living. Then our motivation becomes spiritual. Our every thought grows more Christ-centered.

THE DEEPER LIFE

Scripture declares, *"If in this life only we have hope in*

41

Christ, we are of all men most miserable" (1 Corinthians 1:19).

Again, the apostle Paul reveals that in order to survive we must not just have our faith or commitment to Christ centered only in believing for the earthly, tangible and physical.

Many come to the house of God and see no further than the choir or church building, not receiving spiritual nourishment through the Word of God and the anointing enabling them to destroy yokes that continually arise to obstruct and confuse us.

------------- ♥ -------------

We need a deeper life, a deeper walk
and a deeper revealed truth.

If this does not happen, we will be unhappy and miserable— which is "eleos" in the Greek, meaning uncertain, unstable, wavering, coming and going, unfulfilled in life.

NEEDED: STRONG MEAT!

Here's what I believe is Satan's number one trap. He attempts to stifle our spiritual growth and produce frail, malnourished Christians.

As the Bible tells us, *"For when the time ye ought to be teachers, ye have need that one teach you again which be the first principals of the oracles of God* [precepts or original Christian-teaching how to become a believer]; *and are to become such as have need of milk, and not of strong meat. For*

42

every one that useth [lives on] *milk is unskillful* [underdeveloped in spiritual growth] *in the word or righteousness: for he is a babe* [child]. *But strong meat* [solid revelation knowledge, deeper truth, deeper walk, deeper faith, deeper experiences, deeper acceptance of the Word] *belongeth to them that are of full age* [spiritually mature], *even those who by reason of use have their senses* [faculties] *exercised* [trained] *to discern both good* [God's will] *and evil* [Satan's will]" (Hebrews 5:12-14).

Paul maintains that many are still children in the faith, five, ten and fifteen-year-old spiritual babies who can't do their own thinking. There's no inner, personal relationship with Christ, just outside experiences—nothing rock solid or dependable. They don't rely on the Word, and when a crisis hits, they immediately blame God for not keeping His promises. Such people are fast-food eaters (sermonettes), sleeping till excitement comes through music or the teaching ends.

AVOID THE SHIPWRECK

This is a great danger in the Body of Christ and, as a result, few people are ready for the Lord's return. There is a lack of spiritual maturity, much backsliding and little progress in the understanding of scripture.

What is the solution? I love what Paul says to Timothy: *"Holding faith, and a good conscience; which some having put away concerning faith have made shipwreck"* (1 Timothy 1:19).

We must receive the Word, which comes through anointed preaching and teaching, and hold onto it firmly with a good untouched, untampered conscience. Not a mind where we have failed to listen to God's Word until within us it is seared, dried up and has lost its power to convict or warn us. When we push aside the infallible Word we ruin its effectiveness. The result is a shipwreck—shattered salvation, destroyed spiritual growth and eternal damnation instead of survival and proper development.

The Father has something much greater in store for you.

Let me ask you to pray with me right now:

Lord Jesus, Help me to sustain and maintain my spiritual commitment to You. Make me, through your Word, as you have planned. Lead me to where I can be fed the Word of God. I need revelation knowledge, a deeper truth and a deeper insight.

Let Your anointing be present to destroy any obstacles in my path. Keep me Lord Jesus as I let You direct me into continual growth. For I am an Organism of the Christ Life and I will survive. And nothing and no one will hinder me from being what You desire. In your name, Jesus, I pray. Amen.

CHAPTER 5

"THERE IS NO OTHER LIKE THIS"

Every day, you see billboards or read ads announcing a product or service as: "The Best." "The One and Only." "The Original." "Last Chance." "One in a Million." "Don't Pass This By."

The marketers are trying to persuade, even brainwash you into thinking that if you don't buy or experience what they are promoting, you will sooner or later regret your decision.

One day, as I was driving down the road reading such advertisements, the Lord conveyed this to my spirit-man: "There is no other like this."

God was speaking of Himself, His presence and the relationship He enters into with the believer through salvation, the Holy Spirit and His impartations of love, joy, peace, longsuffering, gentleness, meekness, faith, temperance and goodness, as well as other vital revealing gifts which are available (see 1 Corinthians 12:6-10).

In these last days it is imperative we see and discern this relationship we have entered into with Christ for what it really is. This is a valuable and priceless gift that we must cherish and appreciate. As the Bible has placed direct emphasis on what to expect as a follower of Christ, we must remember every detail. It is a once-in-a-lifetime experience.

NEW WINE!

Let me turn your attention to a scene in Jerusalem. Jews from many nations had gathered to celebrate the Passover—an annual 50-day commemoration of the exodus of the children of Israel from Egypt.

———— ♥ ————

*Suddenly, 120 newly Spirit-filled believers
came pouring out of the Upper Room.*

The people in Jerusalem, *"...were all amazed, and were in doubt, saying one to another, what meaneth this? Others mocking said, these men are full of new wine. But Peter, standing up with the eleven, lifted up his voice, and said unto them, Ye men of Judaea, and all ye that dwell at Jerusalem, be this known unto you, and hearken to my words: For these are not drunken, as ye suppose, seeing it is but the third hour of the day. But this is that which was spoken by the Prophet Joel. And*

46

it shall come to pass in the last days, saith God, I will pour out of my Spirit upon all flesh: and your sons and your daughters shall prophesy, and your young men shall see visions and your old men shall dream dreams" (Acts 2:12-17).

The mighty power of God fell and the Holy Spirit came with dramatic manifestation, so much so that it baffled and astonished those who there from various nations. They heard local men speaking in their native language and wondered, "How could this be?"

That's why Peter, standing with the other 11 disciples, lifted up his voice and explained, "These men are not drunken"—which is the key word in the verse. The observers obviously felt what they were witnessing was the result of people who were intoxicated by strong drink. Yet Peter continued, "There is an influence behind this, but it's not wine."

After all, he explained, this was just the "third hour" (between 9 A.M. and noon), and the taverns weren't open. Rather it was a fulfillment of divine prophecy!

"THIS IS THAT!"

Over 2,000 years earlier, Joel had prophesied that in the last days God would pour out His Spirit upon all flesh. The sons and daughters would predict, foretell and proclaim coming events. God would, by the Spirit, convey to the world through those who were in touch with Him, His work and warnings to a "last day" people.

Peter was announcing, "This is that! There is no other like this. It has arrived and now is the time."

————————— ♥ —————————

*People of God, we must realize that today
we are a living prophecy, a fulfillment of scripture, true
evidence that God's Spirit does dwell on this earth
in a chosen people such as you and I!*

THE "LAYING ON OF HANDS"

We are given not one, but multiple reasons to believe God's Word is able to transform lives. The writer of Hebrews tells us, *"Therefore leaving the principles* [elementary] *of the doctrine of Christ, let us go on unto perfection* [maturity]; *not laying again the foundation of repentance from dead works, and of faith toward God, of the doctrine of baptisms* [Baptism of repentance of sin, baptism by the Holy Ghost into the body of Christ as a member], *and of laying on of hands, and of resurrection of the dead, and of eternal judgment"* (Hebrews 6:1-2).

The "laying on of hands" does not just refer to hands being placed on a person in prayer, but in identifying with the sacrifice which was on the altar. For the Jew had to personally relate to the sacrifice that would die in the place of his sin, thus freeing himself from judgment.

It also pertains to hands being laid on Joshua by Moses at

God's request to elevate him before the people as his successor. (Numbers 27:18, 19). The Levites, too, were offered before God to execute the service of the Lord by the laying on of hands (Leviticus 8:10).

In the New Testament, seven men of honest report, full of the Holy Ghost and wisdom were appointed through this method as the first *deacons* to take care of the church's business (Acts 6:3-6).

Having hands laid on one is sacred, consecrated and holy. We must not treat this as a trivial matter because it is ordained by the mercy of God.

BAPTISM AND REPENTANCE

Regarding the "doctrine of baptisms" Peter declares, *"...baptism doth also now save us (not the putting away of the filth of the flesh, but the answer of a good conscience toward God,) by the resurrection of Jesus Christ"* (1 Peter 3:21).

Continuing in Hebrews 6, we read these extremely important faith-stabilizing verses: *"And this will we do, if God permit. For it is impossible for those who were once enlightened, and have tasted of the heavenly gift, and were made partakers of the Holy Ghost, and have tasted the good word of God, and the powers of the would to come, if they shall fall away, to renew them again unto repentance; seeing they crucify to themselves the Son of God afresh and put him to an open shame"* (Hebrews 6:3-6).

Paul speaks of *repentance*—which is a change of mind, a

49

turning *from* and turning *to* Almighty God.

The Word reveals promises to the penitent and the sorrowful and Isaiah 55:7 and Jeremiah 3:12, 31:9 speaks of forgiveness of sin. Life is extended to us because of a repentant attitude—as in Ezekiel 18:21 and Zechariah 1:3. Prayers are answered, as 2 Chronicles 7:14 states, because of *repentance first*, then prayer.

We cannot continually take advantage of these available gifts over and over again as if they were a freebie. They are too sacred, too special and are the generosity of God's grace and goodness.

RESURRECTION AND JUDGMENT

Paul also writes of the *"resurrection of the dead, and of eternal judgment"* (Hebrews 6:2).

Jesus shows Himself to men as the resurrection itself (John 11:25), and there are many promises to us concerning this (John 5:25, 6:40, Psalm 49:15, Acts 24:15, 2 Corinthians 4:14, and 1 Thessalonians 4:16).

The Bible tells of a Last Judgment awaiting all men: "And as it is appointed unto men once to die, but after this the judgment" (Hebrews 9:27).

There is a judgement *according to privileges* (Mark 6:11; 11:22, Luke 12:48, John 3:19) and judgment *according to works* (Psalms 62:12, Jeremiah 17:10, Matthew 16:27, 2 Corinthians 5:10).

The avenues of extended goodness are only experienced

because God allows it. If we walk away from this blessing and view it as insignificant—something we can casually take or leave—we are seriously jeopardizing our chances with God's goodness, especially after He has made so many options available to His children.

The Word shows us how we have been enlightened: *"To open eyes, and to turn them from darkness to light, and from the power of Satan unto God, that they may receive forgiveness of sins, and inheritance among them which are sanctified by faith that is in me"* (Acts 26:18).

"SET ASIDE"

Praise God! Our eyes are opened and we can see with spiritual, not natural, understanding and insight. We are educated, taught in God's Word and we see His will. God's plan for our lives is made plain and clear. Thus, we are turned from darkness, which is ignorance, no direction and no way out and delivered from Satan's influence and authority over our lives.

———❤———

We've been forgiven of our sins and given a place in God. Blessings await us and we begin to enjoy them.

Even more, the Lord reveals His predestined (pre-planned) blueprint for our future. We see it and are sanctified, set aside for God's purpose by faith (trusting and believing His Word).

51

Hallelujah! The Lord shows us we have tasted of the Heavenly Gift, and have been made partakers of the Holy Ghost. *"Moreover, brethren, I would not that ye should be ignorant, how that our fathers were under the cloud, and all passed through the sea"* [their crossing of the Red Sea]. *And were all baptized unto Moses in the cloud and in the sea, and did all eat the same spiritual meat"* (1 Corinthians 10:1-3).

LIVING WATER

We all have available to us the pure Word of God, His revelation knowledge, His deeper truth, clear insights and how He is always waiting and longing to be received. *"And did all drink the same spiritual drink: for they drank of that spiritual Rock that followed them: and that Rock was Christ"* (v.4).

God satisfied the children of Israel by letting water spring out of the rock when they were in the wilderness and dying of thirst. John 7:38 says, out of our belly, (*koilia* in the Greek, our cavity or hollow place), would flow (rheuo—as water runs) continuous rivers of living water (potamos—drinkable running water). This is a current, unhindered satisfaction of life, joy and fulfillment.

We've experienced the power of the Holy Spirit and we know we cannot purchase these benefits from a department store or catalog. No, He comes from the throne of Glory, at God's bidding, to lead and guide His children into all truth, to reveal the deep things of God, and make Jesus real to our souls.   But after this experience, many of the Israelites did not please God (v.5). For their bodies were scattered in the wilderness where the temperature soared to 130 degrees and mere survival was difficult and uncomfortable. Many times the people rebelled and turned from the Lord because of their dire circumstances. The obstacles overwhelmed those who failed to see that there is no other experience or relationship that can ever compare with that of God. No where. No place. No time! No person!

A DIVINE RELATIONSHIP

Paul says we have *"tasted the good Word of God, and the powers of the world to come"* (Hebrews 6:5)—the very ingredients, essence and substance of life-changing, divine principles. It has been received through preaching, teaching, seminars, sermons, videos, conferences, revivals, crusades, retreats, Bible schools and the Psalms.

Yes, this power we have in our earthen vessels (2 Corinthians 4:7) will one day control completely this earthly realm.

———————♥———————

The old world and its atmosphere will fade and pass away and a new one recreated by God will have supreme control.

People of God, we have this treasure in the Holy Spirit, so if we fall away, backslide or give up, we crucify Christ all over again—and in doing so, we scar our souls and harm the initial work of repentance.

There is a first cry, a breaking which takes place in the soul; a guilty, sorrowful, shameful attitude that causes us to reject sin and turn to God. It produces a heart-felt love for the Lord, an earnest desire to please Him, obey His Word, communicate with and live in His presence through the Holy Spirit.

SATAN'S WEAPON

To give up or lose this heavenly relationship hinders the opportunity to have it recreated. Because it has been tampered and interfered with, it is now a tainted experience. It's like losing your first love; everything else is secondary because of the true, pure love you once shared. Separation causes the believer's life to lose its full impact.

In this vulnerable state, Satan has a greater weapon with which to confront us. Sadly, hearts are hardened toward the Lord, a broken sensitivity occurs and God then renders a second thought instead of an immediate response. As a result, there is the guilt of deliberately and personally sharing in crucifying Christ all over again. It will cause you to put the Christian experience publicly and openly before people who will laugh and mock your so-called relationship. Then, like Peter, the pressure will force you to curse, lie and sink into deeper words of criticism to convince your friends, "It wasn't that much to walk away from anyway," and you'll point fingers of condemnation at "God's people."

This will only give the devil a greater option of demeaning spiritual things to the point where the very memory of God is blasphemed and the five senses (sight, taste, touch, smell, and hearing) take over once again and you are on the level of a sinner.

The difference is that you have personal knowledge and guilt of knowing you left "the most powerful relationship a person could ever enjoy." You have given up God for the carnal world, which will be destroyed. You will face eternal judgment, and all because you walked away.

THROUGH THE ROOF!

Scripture records how Jesus was in a house and there was such a large crowd gathering that people could no longer get through the door (Mark 2:1). Many were there to be ministered to.

One group brought their sick friend on a bed, believing there was no other help for him. Since they were unable to get close to Jesus, they went up on the roof, tore open a hole, and lowered the infirmed man down into the Lord's presence so he could be healed!

———————❤———————

There is no other power, no other
help available to us like God's.

As Jesus declares, *"...the last* [Gentiles] *shall be first, and the first* [Jesus] *last: for many be called* [given the opportunity], *but few chosen* [those who will do what is necessary to withstand the test and go through the challenges]" (Matthew 20:16).

In the days of Joshua, it is described, *"...there was no day like that before it or after it, that the Lord hearkened unto the voice of a man: for the Lord fought for Israel"* (Joshua 10:14).

Joshua respected the relationship he had with God. He honored God's presence, His calling, His Word on his life, and when he needed the Lord, God came through for him.

There is no other like this!

God's power will one day control everything. For every knee shall bow and every tongue confess that Jesus is Lord.

"This is that" which was spoken of. It's here! It's ours! It is real and far too wonderful to let get away!

CHAPTER 6

THAT'S GOD'S PLACE IN ME

In the physical world, there must always be an input before an output:

- A car needs gasoline before it can operate.
- A light bulb must be screwed into the lamp before it gives light.
- A key must be placed into the lock before it will open.
- Food goes into the mouth to be chewed before it can enter the stomach to satisfy hunger.
- Blood must continuously flow through the heart and our major life-sustaining organs to keep us alive.

And spiritually, God must have a place in our heart before we can become alive to Him.

In the beginning, when the Almighty formed man, He said,

"Let us make man in our image, after our likeness: and let them have dominion over the fish of the sea, and over the fowl of the air, and over the cattle, and over all the earth, and over every creeping thing that crept upon the earth. So God created man in his own image, in the image of God created he him, male and female created he them" (Genesis 1:26-27).

———————❤———————

There are two distinct phrases which stand out in this passage: one is "in our image" and the other, "after our likeness."

As the Godhead began to form man, the Creator says, "We will make them male and female in our image," and it appears that God is talking about ears, eyes, noses and lips. However, according to the gospel of John, He is not. We read, *"God is a Spirit: and they that worship him must worship him in spirit* [meaning man's spirit] *and in truth"* (John 4:24).

A "MEETING PLACE"

The Word implies that in order for us to fellowship with God who is a Spirit, man must have the same instruments with which to reach and commune with Him.

So the Almighty first speaks of making man out of the same essence He is comprised of, the image and components of God Himself. Then He adds, *"and after our likeness."* This means

His attributes or functions of operational procedures.

Man was to have a three-fold operation of His existence: body, soul, spirit—a mind, a will and emotions enclosed in his soul. He would also have a body which would house his five senses: feeling, tasting, seeing, smelling, and hearing—all designed for the earth realm.

Last, but greatest of all, man was given a spirit: a meeting place for the very God who created him to enjoy mutual communication. As God the Father, who is the Maker and Sustainer, is united to the Son, who is the Word of God and Jesus our Savior (Deliverer, Intercessor and Advocate in the earth realm, the Spirit of God, the Holy Ghost, our Comforter, our Power, our Keeper and our Communicator), God will target a channel, a mainstream of fellowship. This is where He reveals Himself to fallen man, restoring, regenerating and making him all over again through that place—*God's special place in us.*

"ONE IN SPIRIT"

The Bible declares, *"And the Lord God formed man of the dust of the ground"* (Genesis 2:7). This is the chemical substance, the outer covering of the man. Then He says, *"...and breathed into his nostrils the breath of life."*

Praise God! This does not just mean the Creator simply blew air into the substance He formed, because such a powerful God could have blown to pieces and obliterated the very being He had just created. But what the Word of God is communicating

59

to us in this: God *ventilated* man, just as in the winter time we can control the temperature inside and make it warm even though it might be below zero outdoors. Likewise, when it is hot and humid outside we can regulate the indoor temperature with a thermostat and make our surroundings cool and refreshing.

The Father, in all of His wisdom, was *fixing* man so His spirit could have a place to dwell in the creation He made—making them one in spirit. The very life of God Himself would be functioning in man.

WHERE THE SPIRIT RESIDES

The Bible tells us, *"But the hour cometh, and now is, when the true worshippers shall worship the Father in spirit* [small "s" meaning in man's personal spirit] *and in truth"* (John 4:23).

There would take place a meeting with God's Spirit, resulting in a powerful communication.

————— ♥ —————

This is where the Holy Ghost resides, in the human spirit of man, renewing the sinner's dead spirit giving it the very life of God.

The Word declares, *"Howbeit when he, the Spirit of truth, is come, he will guide you into all truth"* (John 16:13). The Greek word for guide is "krateufino" meaning to "direct, straighten or lead you into all the Word and ways of God."

Then we read, *"...for he shall not speak of himself"* (v.13). That's referring to *communication.* You see, God fellowships with the spirit of the believer in the earth realm. He is the *work* person who empowers: *"...but whatsoever he shall hear, that shall he speak"* (v.13) Where? In the spirit of the believer, which is God's place in you.

Next we learn, *"...and he will show you things to come"* (v.13). That's *revelation*—deeper insight; a warning from God Himself. The key Greek word "photizo" means to brighten up, turn on the lights, allowing the natural to be seen in spiritual essence and being able to understand it. This throws illumination on the soulish nature where the carnal minded, unsaved person follows his or her feelings and thoughts, and then makes a decision based on that alone.

THE THREE "O's"

The Spirit of God, through man's renewed spirit, reveals God, Christ, God's laws, God's desires, God's plans and intentions for that person and this in turn gives him a life-preserving choice rather than a temporal earthly set of options.

Jesus goes on to say, *"He* [the Holy Spirit] *shall glorify me: for he shall receive of mine, and shall show it unto you. All things that the Father hath are mine: therefore said I, that he shall take of mine, and shall show it unto you"* (vv.14-15).

He is telling the disciples that the Holy Spirit is revealing and making clear in the spirit of the believer the relationship of

61

God the Father and God the Son Jesus Christ.

The gifts of the Spirit are to be ministered to the body of Christ through people's renewed spirit and to the souls of men through words of wisdom. This is made possible because of the three O's which are in operation for the born again Christian:

1. God's Omniscience—His vast all-knowing insight which is not limited.
2. God's Omnipresence—His accessibility to be everywhere at the same time.
3. God's Omnipotence—His power, authority, healing, miracles, prophecy, tongues which is for utterance and edification in the believer.

MAN'S "HOLLOW PLACE"

Scripture tells us, *"The spirit of man is the candle of the Lord, searching all the inward parts of the belly"* (Proverbs 20:27). This does not imply God has a literal candle ready to place inside man to visibly inspect his insides. As if to say, "He's looking at my liver, my kidneys, and my stomach."

No. To properly understand, let's read John 7:38: *"He that believeth on me, as the scripture hath said, out of his belly shall flow rivers of living water"*

"Belly" in the Greek means "koilia" which is the hollow place in man, a cavity or void the Spirit of God would fill in man's spirit.

So God reveals insights concerning spiritual things into man's hollow places. The dark areas become light and man's ignorance becomes intelligent—not earthly college-wise, but God-wise, heaven-wise, eternal-wise.

YOU ARE SET APART

On the day of Pentecost, *"...they were all filled with the Holy Ghost"* (Acts 2:4). The Greek word for *filled* is "empletho," which means *satisfied.* Yes, God filled an emptiness, a missing spiritual experience in the hollow cavity of each person. God claimed and possessed a special place in them.

The apostle Paul writes, *"But we are bound to give thanks always to God for you, brethren beloved of the Lord, because God hath from the beginning* [back in Genesis at the creation of man], *chosen you to salvation through sanctification of the Spirit* [God's], *and belief of the truth* [Word of God]" (2 Thessalonians 2:13).

———————❤———————

As we receive the Word of God and believe its truth, the Spirit of God works with our inner man bringing us to a place of salvation, deliverance, redemption, forgiveness, regeneration and justification.

Jesus says, *"Except a man be born of the water and of the Spirit, he cannot enter into the Kingdom of God."* (John 3:6).

63

This is confirmed in Paul's letter to the Ephesians: *"That he might sanctify* [set apart for his own purpose], *and cleanse it with the washing of water by the word"* (Ephesians 5:26).

INNER RENEWAL

We are recreated by God's Spirit—*"...born, not of blood, nor of the will of the flesh, nor of the will of man, but of God"* (John 1:13).

The *Word* of God working with the *Spirit* of God makes a new inward existence of man. He then enters the governing and ruling realm of the Father instead of, as before, being led by impulse, cravings and desires which are created by his five senses and the appetites of his body.

Remember, *"...the Kingdom of God is within you"* (Luke17:21)—meaning the laws of the Almighty.

The "steerage" of the Father takes place internally after a man is delivered, saved, renewed through the Word and Spirit of the Lord.

"That which is born of the flesh is flesh [the earthly physical fallen nature reproduces the same thing]; *and that which is born of the Spirit* [which is God's Spirit] *is spirit"* (John 3:6). Again, the latter is a small "s" meaning *man's* spirit is reborn, made new by God's Spirit entering in and making it according to His will, His ways and His ultimate plan.

REVELATION KNOWLEDGE

I get excited when I read, *"...God, who commanded the light to shine out of darkness, hath shined in our hearts, to give the light of the knowledge of the Glory of God in the Face of Jesus Christ"* (2 Corinthians 4:6).

The same way the Creator spoke and physical light manifested itself in the elements, God Himself has released His revelation knowledge—which is "epiginosis" in the Greek.

This means exact knowledge and perfect wisdom of God revealed into the soulish nature of fallen man, awakening him to the total plan and understanding of what Jesus Christ meant and was to His children in this earth realm. This makes clear and plain what God gave us through Jesus Christ, the Word, made in the likeness of sinful flesh to make it possible for God to dwell in man on the earth—as He planned with Adam, in the original creation.

The Father has a place in which He resides—and that is in the spirit of the believer. Yes, that is God's special place in you.

CHAPTER 7

THE WORKING OF THE WORD ON EARTH

Let me share with you what I consider to be one of the most important and effective ministries of the Holy Spirit available in our time.

What I am speaking of is the working of the Word in the earth realm—a vital key to your internal achievement.

This unique activity represents a great move of the Spirit toward a certain destined and God-willed providence which is God-designed and preplanned. As we will see, it involves the nation of Israel (His chosen people) and the Gentile era which will come to its completion when the prophecy is fulfilled that *"...this gospel of the kingdom shall be preached in all the world for a witness unto all nations; and then shall the end come"* (Matthew 24:14).

THE SPIRIT "MOVED"

As we look at the foundation of this ministry of the Spirit, we see how, *"In the beginning God created the heaven and the earth. And the earth was without form, and void; and darkness was upon the face of the deep. And the Spirit of God moved upon the face of the waters. And God said, Let there be light: and there was light"* (Genesis 1:1-3).

———————❤———————

In the words "the Spirit of God moved" it is evident there is distinct action taking place by God the Father, God the Son and God the Holy Ghost. Three separate personalities in one God, all working together.

A key Greek word for " moved:" is "roo-ukh" which translates as, a fast, noisy breathing or screaming in a violent exertion—getting excited for something to happen.

SPIRITUAL "CLOCKWORK"

The Spirit of God was preparing to get involved in molding and creating a world. This is the same Spirit which moved in the Upper Room when, *"...suddenly there came a sound from heaven as of a rushing mighty wind, and it filled all the house where they were sitting"* (Acts 2:2).

Can you imagine these dramatic manifestations of the Spirit at Pentecost?

Genesis 1:3 begins by saying "And God said." This is not just the Creator speaking words, but it is actually the working of God the Father and God the Son—or the Word—operating in unity, side by side, move by move. In this case, *two* distinct personalities functioning in one accord. Whatever the Father wills, the Word is there, responding to it at the exact same moment. It is spiritual "clockwork," One with One, in perfect step with each other.

In the gospel of John we learn this foundational truth: *"In the beginning was the Word, and the Word was with God, and the Word was God. The same was in the beginning with God"* (John 1:1-2).

The next verse, however, is vital: *"All things were made by him; and without him was not any thing made that was made"* (v.3).

"All things" encompass every work of creation Genesis 1 spoke of—the light (physical and spiritual), the herb-yielding seed, the three heavens (one being the atmospheric heaven; the second is the celestial heaven—the stars, moon and planets; and the third is God's throne room).

THE "LIVING" WORD

The Father, the Word and the Spirit all perform a *heavenly* ministry together, and as the Father wills, the Word and Spirit help establish it.

Yet, there is a "work in the *earth* realm" the Father desires to be accomplished in men's lives. Adam and Eve were created, but they were deceived by Satan who used the serpent—one of the most intelligent creatures God made. Satan mislead the first man and woman and caused them to lose their authority as sin overtook them.

We read, *"And the Lord God said unto the serpent, because thou hast done this, thou are cursed above all cattle, and above every beast of the field; upon thy belly shalt thou go, and dust shalt thou eat all the days of thy life"* (Genesis 3:14).

There was also punishment for Adam and Eve. God declared, *"And I will put enmity* [warfare] *between thee and the woman, and between thy seed and her seed; it shall bruise thy head, and thou shalt bruise his heel"* (v.15).

This speaks of the coming of a Messiah, Christ's sufferings, Satan's ultimate defeat in men's lives followed by the devil's complete annihilation.

————————❤————————

*The Messiah would arrive through the Word
of God and become flesh in the earth appearing
first to a chosen people—the Jews.*

Scripture declares, *"He* [the Word] *came unto his own, and his own received him not"*(John 1:11).

IN THE "FORM" OF GOD

The Ministry of the Word took the human form of a Man named Jesus. *"He* [the Word] *was in the world, and the world was made by him, and the world knew him not"* (v.10). *Him* speaks of the spiritual part of God the Son. *"And the Word was made flesh, and dwelt among us, (and we beheld his glory, the glory as of the only begotten of the Father), full of grace and truth"* (v.14).

A conversation between Jesus and Phillip speaks to the unity of the Father and Son. Jesus asked him, *"Have I been so long with you, and yet hast thou not known me, Phillip? He that hath seen the Father; and how sayest thou then, shows us the Father? Believest thou not that I am in the Father, and the Father in me?"* (John 14:9-10).

Later, the apostle Paul writes of Jesus, *"Who, being in the form of God, thought it robbery to be equal with God? But made himself of no reputation, and took upon him the form of a servant, and was made in the likeness of men"* (Philippians 2:6-7). Jesus was in the *"form"* of God.

This is the Word coming down by the will of the Father to be the only begotten Son in the likeness of sinful flesh (*dulos,* which means a Roman slave, the lowest of lows, being born to serve).

In theological terms this is called the "kenosis theory" where God empowered or poured forth all of His divinity into humanity to meet human need. Again, it is the "the working of the Word in the earth realm." This produced "Theo-Anthropos"—God-Man (*Theo*-God; *Anthropos*-Man).

A DOOR WAS OPENED

How does all this affect our world today?

Paul, writing to the believers at Rome, says, *"(According as it is written, God hath given them the spirit of slumber, eyes that they should not see, and ears that they should not hear;) unto this day. Let their eyes be darkened, that they may not see, and bow down their back alway. I say then, have they stumbled that they should fall? God forbid: but rather through their fall salvation is come unto the Gentiles, for to provoke them to jealousy. Now if the fall of them* [or false step of them] *be the riches of the world, and the diminishing of them* [the nation of Jews] *be the riches of the Gentiles* [every nationality of the world that are not Jews]; *how much more their fullness?"* (Romans 11:8-12).

This passage deals with how the Jews rejected Christ. They simply overlooked Him as the Messiah, and by doing so a "door" was opened to the Gentiles so that salvation would be made available to the *entire* human race. Their mistake was our blessing!

Later in the chapter Paul writes, *"For I would not, brethren, that ye should be ignorant of this mystery, lest he should be wise in your own conceits: that blindness* [spiritual blindness] *in part is happened to Israel, until the fullness of the Gentiles be come* in " (v.25). *"For God hath concluded them all in unbelief, that He might have mercy upon all"* (v.32).

I pray you can see how the Word is actively working in this day and age.

Just think how Jesus Christ, the Word made flesh, was rejected by His chosen people because they were spiritually blind. God suffers it to be so, and salvation was exposed to the rest of the world.

---------❤---------

Today, the Word is being preached to all the earth according to Matthew 24:14 and the time of the Gentiles will be over when the Gospel has reached every nook and city of this planet.

The Word operates in the earth through men and women as carriers of the Gospel.

THE TRANSFORMING WORD

These questions are asked by Paul: *"How then shall they call him in whom they have not believed? And how shall they believe in him of whom they have not heard? And how shall they hear without a preacher? And how shall they preach* [to proclaim God's good news], *except they be sent?"* (Romans 10:14-15).

The nations are reached through those who have been

spiritually transformed. We are told, *"And be not conformed to this world..."* (Romans 12:2).

The *world* is translated "tevel" in the Hebrew, meaning the habitual earth as made for man with all of its natural and tangible resources. "Aion" is the Greek word—meaning temporal of that which exists, and "kosmos," referring to the created order or habits, methods, activities and affairs in an evil sense, against Christ.

However, Paul continues, *"...but be ye transformed by the renewing of your mind"* (v.2). In simple terms, let the Word work in your life so that it converts and changes you, taking you from the influences of the powers of darkness into the Kingdom of Christ Jesus—into spiritual things.

This is accomplished through the renewal of your mind—the soulish nature. It is controlled by revelation knowledge which comes from the Word and is 'birthed" into our spirit man. This influences our decisions, causing us to demonstrate the perfect and acceptable will of God.

What is the reason for this renewal? *"That he might sanctify and cleanse it* [the Church, body of believers, saints)] *with the washing of water by the word"* (Ephesians 5:26).

Christ ("Apo" in the Greek) separates the Church from the world by the working of His Word. It washes and cleanses man spiritually in the earth realm.

This produces internal achievement in us. We advance, bear the fruit of the Word which creates in us the image God wants to show the world through our character, work-activity, relationships and associations.

———————❤———————

We give the world a pattern to follow, a lifestyle to desire, a good relationship with God to pursue internally—which will be seen outwardly.

FIRMLY ROOTED

The most important impact the Word has on earth for the Church is: *"That we henceforth be no more children* [infants, unstable and underdeveloped] *tossed to and fro, and carried about with every wind of doctrine, by the sleight of men* ["taham" in the Greek meaning earthly intelligence, earthly advice, earthly understanding], *and cunning craftiness, whereby they lie in wait to deceive"* (Ephesians 4:14).

The objective is to establish a firmly rooted people who are not leaning to earthly knowledge, but being nurtured and developed by Holy scriptures. As Paul boldly declares, *"For I am not ashamed of the gospel of Christ: for it is the power* [authority, influence] *of God unto salvation to everyone that believeth, to the Jew first, and also to the Greek"* (Romans 1:16).

Thank God for *salvation.* Through that one word, and the Savior it represents, we have deliverance from penalty of sin, redemption, regeneration, conviction, holiness, righteousness, sanctification, justification and reconciliation.

AN INTERNAL LIGHT

There is a verse which sums up this theme so beautifully: *"For God, who commanded the light* [physical-revelation knowledge] *to shine out of darkness, hath shined in our hearts* [the soulish nature], *to give the light* [revelation knowledge/deeper understanding about God; raw, untouched, fresh insight] *of the knowledge* [insight] *of the glory of God in the face of Jesus Christ"* (2 Corinthians 4:6).

Praise the Lord! The Word is wonderfully alive and working right now to make a spiritually complete, God-fearing and a prepared people for Christ to come back and rapture (catch away) from all nations, creeds and colors.

In God's glorious message to man is life eternal, yet there is a time limit set by the Almighty for man to respond. No one knows the hour of His return. Are you ready?

CHAPTER 8

LOOKING IN THE MIRROR OF YOUR HEART

E very successful person I have met has at least one of several things going for them. Either they have been in the company of other high achievers, they were taken under the wing of a mentor, or they searched deep within their heart and—like a mirror—saw who they were and what they could become.

Thank God for those who recognize the abilities and talents of others and are willing to share of their time and knowledge to help shape the future of someone with a sharp mind and a keen perception. When you are willing to be a student, there is always a teacher. And the ultimate Tutor is God Himself.

This Instructor never abandons His student, doesn't hide or shade the truth and brings much needed wisdom to the classroom. The teaching never ends and there are no other students to interfere or vie for His personal attention. The instruction is always available and ready to be poured into listening ears.

Internal achievement is realized by constantly coming in contact with this divine Teacher.

A REFLECTION OF THE REAL YOU

The word *heart* is used in the Bible to explain the workings of the mind—including our thinking, reasoning, ideas, considerations, choices, decisions and conclusions one eventually arrives at and makes.

———❤———

As we will see, scriptures relate to what can help or hurt an internal achiever. They reveal the heart as a mirror, showing us who we are, where we are and how to move to another level.

A mirror serves the purpose of reflection, showing the same object, not a different one which enters into its space. Nothing is deleted and nothing is added. The complete visual image is echoed, reproduced and instantly flashed back for us to see.

"EVIL IMAGINATIONS"

According to God's Word, the thoughts of our heart can land us in deep trouble.

After sin entered the world, *"...God saw that the wickedness* [evil or morally bad choices, mean, spiteful, troublesome or dangerous, unrighteous, blasphemous, corrupt] *of man* [mankind] *was great in the earth, and that every imagination of the thoughts of his heart was only evil continually"* (Genesis 6:5).

The imagination—*yasar* in Hebrew—refers to something formed and created in the mind. In this case, the "thoughts of the heart" were "only" (exclusively) evil—unholy and harmful.

As a result, *"...it repented the Lord that he had made man on the earth, and it grieved him at his heart. And the Lord said, I will destroy man whom I have created from the face of the earth; both man, and beast, and the creeping thing, and the fowls of the air; for it repenteth me that I have made them"* (vv.6-7).

THE SOURCE OF THE PROBLEM

When the eyes of God searched back and forth across the land, the activity of mankind had deteriorated to the point that nothing being done reflected His perfect will and principles. It was all iniquity and deception.

The real source of the problem was man's heart—and his mind, will and emotions showed no hope, no desire or motivation to change. The invisible mirror inside was so clouded by sin it was unreachable.

This gives us just a glimpse of how powerful, persuasive and controlling the heart really is. So much so that God decided, "I must destroy all of these people. There is no hope—no future!"

THE WELLSPRING OF ACHIEVEMENT

What a difference it makes when the same instrument—the heart—is properly responded to and followed. It's the secret source of internal achievement.

Jesus declared, *"...for out of the abundance of the heart the mouth speaketh"* (Matthew 12:34). And He added, *"A good man out of the good treasure of the heart bringeth forth good things: and an evil man out of the evil treasure bringeth forth evil things"* (v.35).

Every aspect of life points to the heart—including our conversation and behavior.

————————❤————————

What is visibly demonstrated on the outside, begins as hidden on the inside. It is the wellspring of all accomplishment and achievement.

THOUGHTS OF THE HEART

Perhaps we need to see the value of our heart as the Lord does. A place to store the "good treasures" of life—the gems and jewels which can never be replaced. However, this storehouse can be used for both good and evil, plus it is place of persuasion which affects all of our actions.

Some would argue it is only our mind which controls our behavior, but according to scripture, *"For as he thinketh in his heart so is he"* (Proverbs 23:7). Yes, the thoughts you harbor in the depths of your heart determine the real you!

Few have ever succeeded without being influenced by the *thoughts* and *desire* of achievement. This is what propels the effort necessary and the focus required to accomplish goals.

If you truly want to see where you are headed in God's divine plan, keep looking in the mirror of your heart.

CHAPTER 9

IT'S DAYLIGHT SAVINGS TIME

The term "Daylight Savings Time" is used every year as the sun moves higher in our hemisphere and there is a longer availability of light. The daytime hours are lengthened and the need for artificial illumination is reduced.

When this happens, clocks are reset so we can take full advantage of the sun.

Just as man prepares and looks forward to the extended time span of the earth's light, God also has a "saving plan" that involves His "Son."

SPIRITUALLY BLIND

As I was thinking about this truth, my attention turned to the story in the book of John concerning the man who was blind from birth.

When Jesus and His disciples were passing by, they noticed this individual and the disciples asked Him, *"Master, who did sin, this man, or his parents, that he was born blind? Jesus answered, neither hath this man sinned, nor his parents: but that the works of God should be made manifest in him. I must work the works of him that sent me, while it is day: the night cometh, when no man can work. As long as I am in the world, I am the light of the world"* (John 9:2-5).

The man who Jesus observed was sightless, existing in the "black of night" all of his days, unable to see his surroundings or delight in life's grand view. Darkness is symbolic of spiritual blindness—a lacking of insight pertaining to the things of God.

SEEING WHAT IS AVAILABLE

I am convinced there are untold thousands upon thousands who love the Lord and are born again, but remain spiritually "in the dark," unable to receive the deeper truth and fuller revelation of God's Word. It's not a matter of personal failure which is the problem, rather, the works of God have not been made manifest in them. They have not welcomed or embraced the gifts of the Spirit including, wisdom, knowledge, faith, healing, miracles, prophecy, spiritual utterance and discernment of spirits

All these are gifts from God to man through His Spirit which indwells the believer. Yet, Jesus says, "I am the light"—which allows you to see what is available.

NIGHT IS COMING!

Jesus explains that He can only *"work the works"* (v.4)

84

while it is day, meaning the season of time determined by God.

Christ, the "revelation knowledge" of the Almighty, operates while this same " revelation knowledge" is made available to men. He warns "the night cometh," which is symbolic of the lost opportunities which keep presenting themselves to us.

Those struggling in total ignorance need the truth of the Gospel revealed to their hearts.

---------- ♥ ----------

Jesus says when darkness falls, no man can work the works of God. For this reason, while it is still day, we need a deeper faith to bring total deliverance.

Christ is held back, and so are we—in that we are living in a trying time and must take advantage of the Word which is being made known today. While we have spiritual "Daylight Savings Time," we must be awake to the vision and dream God is making available to us through His Word and by the Holy Spirit.

THE "REVEALER"

The disciples asked, "Who did sin?" In other words, who violated God's Holy Word? Who is out of the will of God?

Jesus answered that the fault didn't lie with either the blind man or his parents. Rather, it happened because the works of God needed to be made manifest in this sightless man.

What a contrast between a person stumbling in the darkness and Jesus, who proclaims, "I am the light." Here was the Revealer, communicating to this man, "As long as I am here, I am continually functioning as the light, making the works of God clearer and more perceivable to men."

FOR A SEASON

To better understand God's Daylight Savings Time, let me turn your attention to what happened at Creation: *"And God saw the light, that it was good: and God divided the light from the darkness"* (Genesis 1:3).

The word *light* is mentioned twice in this verse. The first in the Greek is "photizo," meaning to shed rays, to shine or brighten. The second is "phaino"—to appear or to be seen.

God also declared, *"Let there be lights* [stars] *in the firmament of the heaven* [outer space] *to divide the day from the night; and let them be for signs, and for season, and for days, and years: And let them be for lights in the firmament of the heaven to give light upon the earth: and it was so. And God made two great lights* [the sun and the moon]; *the greater light to rule the day* [the sun], *and the lesser light to rule the night* [the moon]: *he made the stars also. And God set them in the firmament of the heaven to give light upon the earth, and to rule over the day and over the night, and to divide the light from the darkness: and God saw that it was good"* (vv.14-18).

————— ♥ —————

*In the natural, it appears that "light" and "day"
are just physical illuminations for man's environment,
but the scripture is also unveiling a spiritual light
which is being released at the same time.*

IT'S STILL DAYTIME!

When God is separating light from darkness in the natural sense (v.4), He is also dividing spiritual light for us which is revelation knowledge—perfect exact wisdom and insight of scripture. This makes God's will clearly discernable to all, as opposed to darkness, which includes ignorance, lack of preparation, being unlearned, and blind.

In an earth which was void, shapeless and had no substance, the first thing God does is, through light, to make a way to visibly see what He is about to form—and make it possible for man to visually enjoy His creation.

So, we have the spiritual "light" (revelation knowledge) and the "day" (opportunity).

Friend, we need the Almighty to impart to us and make clear His will while it is still day and while opportunities are made available to us. Just as physical light directs the time of our days, God's vast knowledge and deeper truths allow us to properly take advantage of every opportunity He presents.

Night (directed by the lesser light, a reflection of the sun called the moon) is symbolic of limited understanding and only partial spiritual sight.

As is evident all around us, men and women in our time call on God and receive from Him in the manner they know Him.

———————❤———————

Limited light means limited knowledge and
small understanding equates to small insight.

Because of this, the person who fails to receive the "Light" is hampered, knowing only a portion of the glory of Jesus Christ and, as a result are not close to God as He desires.

But the Father, from the beginning, was making provision for His Son (the Word) to come from heaven to mankind to make the Father God plain and clear: *Olam*—The Everlasting God; *Elohim, Yahweh.*

HOW MUCH LONGER?

I marvel at the precise planning of our Creator. For example, the earth takes a year to revolve around the sun, but the sun takes approximately 200 million years to make one revolution around the center of the Milky Way. During this period, the sun travels in excess of 10 billion times as far as the distance between it and the earth. All this time the sun is giving off white, brilliant light—pure and clear.

While the sun takes millions of years to reveal its light through God's created order, spiritually, we have only a short time to receive from the vastness of Jesus Christ who is the express image of God to man. As scripture records, it is *"for signs, and for seasons, and for days, and years"* (Genesis 1:14).

I pray you realize that because of the sin and degradation which is swirling around believers, the goodness of God toward earth will not continue forever.

The days and years are passing by, yet even now the Lord is still disclosing deeper truth, purpose and eternal life to mankind. He does this through the scriptures, the shed blood of His Son Jesus Christ and the presence of the Holy Spirit.

"MOVE WITH GOD'S MOVING"

The moon is the brightest object in the night sky and the earth's nearest neighbor in space, yet it gives off no light of its own. So when the moon shines, it is reflecting or casting back light from the sun. Some nights it appears as a gleaming silver globe and other evenings it shines as a thin slice of light.

I want you to understand this in a spiritual sense. Night represents darkness, the time when there is light but only *assisted* illumination, not bright original light (revelation knowledge) from the Son, Jesus Christ. Yet there is still a reflection of the Son into the ignorance, blindness, and unspiritual areas of lives.

The Bible says men would love darkness because their deeds were evil. This is why God sent His Son to earth. *"That was the true Light, which lighteth every man that cometh into the world"* (John 1:9).

Christ is being made known to every man's mind, consciousness and heart. But we must move with *God's* moving. As Jesus declares, *"...yet a little while is the light with you. Walk while ye have the light, lest darkness come upon you: for he that walketh in darkness knoweth not whither he goeth"* (John 12:35).

He is telling you to follow God's path as it is revealed to you—and while the opportunities are present. Remember, the revelation knowledge that God is sending is temporal. The sacrifice of Christ is completed.

THE LIGHT STILL SHINES

Today, salvation is available; plus prophecy and all of the nine manifestations of the gifts of the Spirit are functioning on earth. But time is drawing to a close.

It is your Heavenly Father, *"Who coverest thyself with light as with a garment"* (Psalms 104:2). Yes, God Himself is light, (insight, spiritual education, revelation, deeper understanding). And, *"... in thy light shall we see light"* (Psalm 36:9).

We will *never* understand spiritual things (nor can we) until we submit to the path God places before us. And, as we follow His direction and are led by His Spirit, a deeper knowledge and reality of what the Lord has designed comes into focus. Now we are ready to function in God's laws and desires.

Paul, writing to the believers at Corinth, says, *"But if our gospel be hid, it is hid to them that are lost: In whom the god of this world* [Satan] *hath blinded* ["skia" in the Greek, meaning to put a shade, shadow, or darkness over their understanding and "prosis" meaning blindness, to render stupid or callous] *the minds of them which believe not, lest the light* [revelation knowledge] *of the glorious gospel of Christ, who is the image* ["ikon," meaning copy, representation, likeness] *of God, should shine unto them. For God, who commanded the light to shine out of darkness, hath shined in our hearts, to give the light of the knowledge of the glory of God in the face of Jesus Christ"* (2 Corinthians 4:3-6).

Praise God!

---------------❤---------------

Just as the Creator ordered natural,
physical light rays to break through the sky
and shine, He sent His Son to make clear His
truth, His person, His will and His plans.

They are presented by the Gospel and made discernable to men, through the light of Christ.

RESTORING THE BROKEN-HEARTED

At the start of Jesus' earthly ministry, He went to the synagogue and was given the book of the Law from which to read. Quoting from the prophet Isaiah, He read, *"The Spirit of the Lord is upon me, because he hath anointed me to preach the*

91

gospel to the poor; he hath sent me to heal the brokenhearted, to preach deliverance to the captives, and recovering of sight to the blind, to set at liberty them that are bruised, to preach the acceptable year of the Lord" (Luke 4:18-19).

God's presence and anointing was, and is, alive and well in the earth. The message of the Gospel must reach the poverty-stricken areas of our lives. It will bring healing and restore the devastation of a broken heart, a wounded spirit and frayed emotions.

————— ♥ —————

The message of Christ gives release from a disappointed relationship or a shattered trust. It makes possible deliverance, freedom and liberty for the captives—those who are no longer in control of their lives.

For those whose vision of God is blurred, impaired or totally gone, He brings sight through revelation knowledge.

Christ sets free all who are guilt-ridden and disfigured from the ugly, unattractive things they can't face—including drugs, alcohol and the detestable areas of rape, incest and molestation.

These reflect man's most vital needs and also his major excuses of why he has no relationship with the Father. But thank God, through His Son, through opportunities (day) and through light (revelation knowledge), there shines into the night and darkness (ignorant and unreached areas of men's lives) a bright and shining answer.

The Gospel is being proclaimed, not just in a sermon, but by life (*zoe*-God's life) and victory. The Lord gives us a way out and a chance to recover.

THE TIME IS NOW!

The Bible tells us, *"To every thing there is a season, and a time to every purpose under the heaven"* (Ecclesiastes 3:1).

It's Daylight Saving Time. Don't let God's moment of heavenly knowledge pass you by, for when night comes, no man can work.

Increase your efforts, lengthen your attention span and receive every word God speaks to your mind and heart, because the time is short and we are in the last hour.

Christ is quickly placing Himself into position to return for His church. If we don't move when it is *time* to move, it will be too late.

CHAPTER 10

INTERNAL ACTIVITY ON EXTERNAL DISPLAY

M oses experienced it. So did David. And you can too!

We can have such a glorious transformation on the inside that it impacts everything we do. Internal achievement is the result of what is at work within us—unseen, hidden and out of sight.

In reality, however, this invisible activity is so powerful it cannot remain forever concealed. At some point it becomes part of our behavior and is presented to the world, visibly and physically.

God has placed a computer chip inside each of us that will outperform anything Intel or IBM can ever design. Your mind has the unique ability to store millions of pieces of data—every thought we have ever had, or will have! It can't be seen by the human eye, but on a moment's notice, what our brain contains can be transferred into spoken word or demonstrated by our actions.

Talk with any skilled painter or sculptor and they will probably tell you, "I have to mentally visualize the finished product before I can create a piece of art."

Productivity, accomplishment and success begins with choices and decisions we make deep inside. Only when this happens is there a chance for outward results.

LET YOUR HEART LEAD

You've heard it said, "You can't judge a book by its cover" —and it's true.

---♥---

Some of the most unlikely heroes of history became high achievers, not because of their physical stature, but because of the giant residing within them.

Jonathan, the son of King Saul, knew what it meant to see an invisible victory. One day, while he was with his father and six hundred Israeli soldiers, he said to his armor bearer, "Let's go over to the Philistine garrison patrol on the other side of the pass." However, he didn't breathe a word to his father, King Saul!

"It may be that the Lord will work for us," commented Johnathan, *"...for there is no restraint to the Lord to save by many or few"* (1 Samuel 14:6). He felt there was no cut and dry

rule which says God can only bring deliverance through the force of a huge army. If the Lord is on your side, anything can happen! *"If God be for us, who can be against us?"* (Romans 8:31).

The armor bearer ("kalah"–meaning to cause, accomplish or bring to pass) said to Jonathan, *"Do all that is in thine heart: turn thee; behold, I am with thee according to thy heart"* (1 Samuel 14:7).

In his inner man, Jonathan could picture victory ahead. And now he was *doubly* convinced because he and his friend were in one accord—he had a support system.

These two Jewish soldiers not only walked into the enemy camp, but when the Philistines attacked, God gave them extraordinary *external* strength. The Bible records that in this bloody encounter, Jonathan and his armor bearer slew the garrison of twenty men (v.14). But it set off such confusion among the Philistines, Saul's army was able to enter the camp and finish the job.

THE EYES OF FAITH

Later, when David faced mighty Goliath, he too saw the outcome of the battle before it ever began—not with his physical sight, rather with the "insight" of his soul.

What an amazing moment it must have been when this young man, armed with only a slingshot and five smooth stones, boldly spoke to the giant, declaring, *"This day will the Lord deliver thee into mine hand; and I will smite thee, and I will give the carcasses of the host of the Philistines this day unto the fowls of the air, and to the wild beasts of the earth; that all the earth may know that there is a God in Israel, and all this assembly shall know that the Lord saveth not with sword and spear: For the battle is the Lord's, and he will give you into our hands"* (1 Samuel 17:46).

Through the eyes of faith, David sees how the battle will end. He has an inner-picture of himself representing God and the nation of Israel—and all the Philistines being driven into their hands.

David not only speaks what he sees, he *expects* to experience everything the Lord has shown him—and that's precisely what took place. Goliath *was* defeated and the Philistines were conquered.

THE SIGN OF VICTORY

We also see invisible activity on external display when the armies of Amalek came to fight the children of Israel in the wilderness.

While Joshua led an army forward to battle the Amalekies, Moses, Aaron and Hur went to the top of a hill to watch the events unfold. Even though Moses had strong internal belief, the Lord was about to use a visible, external sign to bring about victory. Scripture tells us, *"... when Moses held up his hand, that Israel prevailed: and when he let down his hand Amalek prevailed. But Moses hands were heavy, and they took a stone and put it under him and he sat thereon; and Aaron and Hur stayed up his hands, the one on one side, and the other on the other side; and his hands were steady until the going down of the sun"* (Exodus 17:11-12).

Moses was demonstrating God's power, not his own—and the armies of Amalek were defeated.

THROUGH OUR "MIND'S EYE"

Regardless of the task ahead, you must have an inward understanding of the project before you can physically or tangibly perform the job well.

Before children ever take their first steps, they observe others and think to themselves, "I can do that, too!" They may stumble and fall a thousand times, but they keep practicing until before you know it they are walking.

Successful basketball players love to tell how they rehearse shooting free-throws over and over in their mind. They believe if you can sink a basket with your eyes closed you can certainly do it with your eyes open!

———————❤———————

What our mind commits to memory is recorded on the canvas of our soul. Then our hands perform what our mind tells them to do.

When God moves upon your heart, there can be no room for failure. What is seen on the inside must be received and believed. As Jesus declares, *"What things soever ye desire, when ye pray, believe that ye receive them, and ye shall have them"* (Mark 11:24)..

The *vision* of accomplishment precedes the mission of success. We see the results through the "mind's eye."

What exciting achievement are you envisioning today?

CHAPTER 11

ONE WORD AT A TIME

As we look at the church today, it is apparent there is a deficiency of spiritual growth and development—especially in people who have been Christians for many years.

Among these believers, surprisingly, there is an amazing lack of knowledge regarding supernatural things, including a misconception of the gifts of the Spirit and a fear of prophecy. They have lost the dynamic power the apostles experienced, even though it is still available through the Holy Spirit at this very hour.

The result is an out-of-date mentality instead of an updated reality.

DO WE REALLY KNOW HIM?

We have not esteemed God's Word as we should because we have not properly understood the operation and the purpose of scripture, nor its potential to influence our daily lives. There is a visible, missing effectiveness of spiritual things.

Do we really long to know and experience God's wisdom, knowledge, prophecy and discerning? Have we established a personal relationship and communion with the God who knows:

- Every mind and every spirit?
- Every relationship and all situations?
- All questions and all answers?
- All thoughts, feelings and desires?
- Every unmentioned secret?

Do we really have fellowship with the One who understands all things—visible and invisible—in earth, in space, in time, in life, in death, in good or evil, in heaven and hell?

————————❤————————

Through God's eternal Word we can know
the Father and understand all of these mysteries.

The prophet Daniel writes, *"And, behold, a hand touched me, which set me upon my knees and upon the palms of my hands. And he said unto me, O Daniel, a man greatly beloved, understand the words that I speak unto thee, and stand upright: for unto thee am I now sent. And when he had spoken this word unto me, I stood trembling. Then said he unto me, Fear not, Daniel: for from the first day that thou didst set thine heart to understand and to chasten thyself before thy God, thy words were heard, and I am come for thy words. But the prince of the kingdom of Persia withstood me one and twenty days. But, lo, Michael, one of the chief princes, came to help me; and I remained there with the kings of Persia. Now I am come to make thee understand what shall befall thy people in the latter days: for yet the vision is for many days."* (Daniel 10:10-14).

It is significant that the angel asks Daniel if he understands the "words"—plural, with an "s."

Then there is a switch in the conversation. It changes from the angel's "words" to God's "word." The angel says, *"...for unto thee am I now sent. And when he had spoken this 'word'..."*

JUST ONE WORD!

Our vocabulary consists of a language which contains different "words" we use to describe or explain whatever we desire to communicate to our listener. But God can utter just *one* "word," and it is filled with His total knowledge of everything in this world—every reaction, every pending circumstance that can or has arisen whether it be past, present or future.

Then, in the above passage, the angel says to Daniel, *"from the first day that thou didst set thine heart to understand and to chasten thyself before thy God, thy words..."* There's that "s" again—meaning more than one word. This tells us Daniel had to use many words and phrases to "cry out" to God. The angel says, *"I am come for thy words,"* which are many.

103

———————— ❤ ————————

*The Word of God is called as such
because every single word is important.*

If you were to read it "word by word," you would realize every syllable has authority and purpose: "Behold!" "A!" "Hand!" "Touched!" "Me!"

Jesus tells us, *"Till heaven and earth pass, one jot or one tittle shall in no wise pass from the law, till all be fulfilled"* (Matthew 5:18).

The "jot" Christ spoke of is the smallest letter in the Hebrew alphabet.

THE WORD CAME THROUGH!

In the Old Testament, King Jehosaphat is told of a great host of warriors who were approaching. So he prepares himself and the people to seek the Lord and ask for His help. In the story we read this conversation where Jehosaphat says, *"...for we have no might against this great company that cometh against us; neither know we what to do: but our eyes are upon thee"* (2 Chronicles 20:12).

Does this sound familiar to you? It certainly does to me! How many times have we been in situations we were virtually unable to handle and desperate to know what to do? We used every noun, verb and prepositional phrase to describe what we were going through.

But wait! God's Word—with infinite knowledge and wisdom—came through for the people. A chosen vessel of the Almighty stood up and opened his mouth. The *Word* of the Lord was spoken aloud, full of divine direction—including a word of knowledge, word of wisdom and prophecy at the same time.

Jahaziel told the people, *"Be not afraid* [consultation], *nor dismayed by reason of this great multitude; for the battle is not yours, but God's* [prophecy]. *Tomorrow go ye down against them: behold* [divine direction, word of knowledge and word of wisdom, all in this verse], *they come up by the cliff of Ziz* [word of knowledge]; *and ye shall find them at the end of the brook, before the wilderness of Jeruel* [divine direction, prophecy]. *Ye shall not need to fight in this battle* [prophecy]: *set yourselves, stand ye still, and see the salvation of the Lord with you* [divine direction, prophecy], *O Judah and Jerusalem: fear not, nor be dismayed; tomorrow go out against them: for the Lord will be with you* [divine direction, prophecy, word of knowledge, and word of wisdom]" (vv.15-17).

RESTORING AND PURIFYING

The psalmist prays, *"...deliver me according to thy word"* (Psalm 119:170)—or according to His vast knowledge of all things.

God has every technique, every insight, every idea and every solution because He knows the totality of the universe. Jesus declares, *"Now ye are clean through the word which I have spoken unto you"* (John, 15:3).

That makes me want to shout!

The precious Word contains so much of God's wisdom, revelation and vast insight it completely reveals every option and method of restoring and purifying the believer's life.

I love what Peter writes concerning this matter: *"Seeing ye have purified your souls in obeying the truth through the Spirit* [God] *unto unfeigned love of the brethren, see that ye love one another..."* (Peter 1:22).

This verse speaks of the power and performance of the word *purify.* It causes separation and filters out the impure areas of our life so we can be renewed and recreated through God's unlimited knowledge. *"Being born again, not of corruptible seed, but incorruptible, by the word of God, which liveth and abideth forever"* (v.23).

AUTHORITY IS RELEASED

A child receives through the seed of his or her parents various motivations, talents, attitudes, character traits—a combination of the two personalities and influences. Likewise, when the Word of God in the life of the believer is followed and submitted to, it causes him to be "born again." The person becomes a "new creature."

The Word not only brings salvation, but releases healing, health and restoration. *"He sent his word, and healed them, and delivered them from their destructions"* (Psalm 107:20). Let those words penetrate your very being. Scripture cures and divinely medicates you in the midst of devastation and disappointment.

———————❤———————

Whether it be through preaching or teaching, God's Word releases authority. So much so that demon spirits recognize its power and flee.

The Son of God, *"...cast out the spirits with his word, and healed all that were sick"* (Matthew 8:16).

THE CENTURION'S FAITH

Once, when Jesus was in Capernaum, a Roman centurion had a servant who was near death. The man had such faith, he asked the Lord, *"...but say in a word, and my servant shall be healed"* (Luke 7:7).

The centurion wasn't asking for a lecture or a discourse about healing. He knew just one command from Jesus was all that was necessary.

There is power in whatever the Lord speaks. For example, if God says "stand," that one word is so filled with His knowledge of the past, present and the future it causes any chains which bind you to be broken. It allows you to stand and *withstand* against any opposition.

THE LIVING VOICE OF GOD

The consistent, daily reading of scripture will cause the truth to come alive inside of you. No longer will the verses be seen as mini-sermons, but the living, breathing voice of God—planting His principles and precepts in your heart. They are now stored, ready for when you need them most, whether for joy, comfort, healing, wisdom or encouragement.

His Word gives you the authority to build a future which will withstand the winds of doubt and the storm of defeat.

Make a commitment to study and internalize God's message to man—one word at a time!

CHAPTER 12

UNDERSTANDING A REVELATION

I remember the moment well.

It was a cold Milwaukee night, December 18, 1993, and while driving home I began to pray and thank God for His Spirit in my life—and for so many other blessings. I can still hear myself saying, "Lord give me a complete understanding of what I am to be doing right now in the ministry, in my life and among Your people."

No sooner had I uttered those words when the Spirit of God began to deal with me concerning *"understanding a revelation."* The Holy Spirit actually spoke these words to me.

The Greek word "epiginosi" means to receive exact knowledge or the intended insight that is attached to the Words of God.

Through divine revelation, the Word is made plain and we are able to totally understand and have full insight—so that nothing is hidden or concealed.

WHO AM I?

The Holy Spirit turned my attention to several passages of scripture which demonstrate how man receives a revelation from God.

One day, when Jesus was having a conversation with His disciples near Cesarea Philippi, He asked them, *"Whom do men say that I the Son of man am?"* (Matthew 16:13).

They answered, *"Some say that thou art John the Baptist: some, Elias* [Elijah]*; and others, Jeremias, or one of the prophets"* (v.14). Then Jesus asked the question once more, *"But whom say ye that I am?"* (v.15).

Simon Peter spoke up and gave this answer: *"Thou are the Christ, The Son of the Living God. And Jesus answered and said unto him, Blessed art thou, Simon Barjona, for flesh and blood hath not revealed it unto thee, but my Father which is in Heaven"* (vv.16-17).

In the Living Bible this passage reads, *"'God has blessed you, Simon, Son of Jonah,' Jesus said, 'for my Father in heaven has personally revealed this to you—this is not from any human source.'"*

Recognizing the purposes and reasons for different ministries, gifts and talents is extremely important. When there is no understanding we respond only in our pragmatic minds and quickly began to criticize and compare and can miss out on why

God has chosen a certain person, event or object.

If we ask the Lord, He will personally disclose the answer to the question, "Who do you say I am?"

If we allow God, He will properly reveal to us who He is.

When certain events are happening in our lives people cross our paths at particular times, there is a purpose and a reason.

Before Peter answered, the other disciples said, "Some say that You are John the Baptist"—yet He is not John; there is only one John the Baptist. Then, "Some say You're Jeremias"—but He was not him, since Jeremias had a different purpose and reason for being here, something else to impart from God—a God of variety.

OPEN YOUR EYES

The heart of God is broken when we fail to recognize His revelation.

The Bible tells when Jesus came near the city of Jerusalem, *...he beheld the city and wept over it, saying if thou hadst known, even thou at least in this thy day, the things which belong unto thy peace! But now they are hid from thine eyes"* (Luke 41:42).

The people of the Holy City had missed the promised Messiah because of their closed minds and hard hearts.

———❤———

Christ was crying because He knew what the people would face in the days ahead.

Many do not fulfill what God desires to achieve in their life—the freedom, healing, insight and the relationship with Him. As a result, they do not experience the reality of God.

Countless believers attend a church service, but fail to benefit from the ministry offered. They hear the Word, yet do not receive the teaching necessary to strengthen their faith-walk with the Lord.

Unless we understand the purpose the Almighty has chosen for us, we will continually judge and criticize—and overlook the vital, important move of the Spirit of God!

The Bible declares, *"To everything there is a season and a time to every purpose under the heaven"* (Ecclesiastes 3:1).

Every creation of God is formed uniquely, with individual time schedules and certain events scheduled to happen at particular points. There are special designated moments in the life cycle—whether it be the puberty of young men and women or the budding blossoms on an apple tree.

"FOR SUCH A TIME AS THIS"

The understanding of a revelation the Lord makes available to you can be imperative to your survival.

In the dramatic story of Esther, a young Jewish girl became a queen in Persia. The king, however, had no idea she was Jewish. At a pivotal point, when a plot to kill all the Jews was being planned, her uncle, Mordecai, told Esther, *"For if thou altogether holdest thy peace at this time, then shall there enlargement and deliverance arise to the Jews from another place; but thou and thy father's house shall be destroyed: and who knoweth whether thou art come to the kingdom for such a time as this?* (Esther 4:14).

This was an unusual assignment. If Esther refused or didn't respond properly, she would suffer and a multitude of people (who would benefit from her obeying God) would be lost. The Almighty would have to raise up someone else.

Like Esther, I believe you are situated where you are by the intervention and placing of the hand of the Lord. He has personally selected you "for such a time as this."

———————❤———————

There are blessings the Father has intended for His children, but because they miss God's reason for His plan, the opportunity is lost.

Fortunately, Esther received the message from the Lord and her people were spared.

LIFE-SUSTAINING DIRECTIONS

Through a direct revelation, God can give you specific instructions not available through any other means.

According to scripture, here is what happened to the prophet Elijah. *"And the word of the Lord came unto him, saying, Get*

113

thee hence, and turn thee eastward, and hide thyself by the brook Cherith, that is before Jordan. And it shall be, that thou shalt drink of the brook; and I have commanded the ravens to feed thee there. So he went and did according unto the word of the Lord: for he went and dwelt by the brook Cherith, that is before Jordan" (1 Kings 17:2-6).

What a miracle! The ravens brought him food every morning and evening—and he drank from the stream.

Elijah was given life-sustaining directions from God in a time of famine! The Lord told the prophet exactly where to go: "Don't head south, north or west or you won't survive. Turn east!"

———————♥———————

God was saying, "Do not ask anyone else about the matter, just listen to and rely on Me. And don't stop at any other brook except Cherith" — which means "a place of separation and hiding."

Ravens are unclean birds, scavengers who forage and eat anything. Yet The Lord assured the prophet, "I have spoken to the birds and given them instructions. They will find you and bring you sustenance."

God gives specific instructions for certain things to happen—and they will not occur anywhere else—through any other source.

Elijah believed and received the revelation and he was

miraculously provided for during the famine.

ONLY A "JAWBONE"

Your back may be up against the wall, yet the Lord can show you how to fight the enemy and be victorious.

Think about Samson. He was bound hands and feet and delivered to the Philistines, when suddenly, *"...the spirit of the Lord came mightily upon him, and the cords that were upon his arms became as flax that was burnt with fire, and his bands loosed from off his hands"* (Judges 15:14).

God then showed him specifically how to defeat his adversary. Samson reached down and picked up *"...a new jawbone of an ass, and put forth his hand, and took it, and slew a thousand men therewith"* (v.15).

If he had attempted to use a sword, a tree limb or a knife at this particular moment, he would not have prevailed. But God directed Samson to use the "jawbone"—and no other weapon would have worked.

It is important to let God release His all-knowing power into your life so you can benefit from what He has placed in your path.

WRESTLING WITH AN ANGEL

Don't be surprised if your revelation includes a face-to-face encounter with God.

Jacob, frighted at the prospect of a visit from his angry

brother, Esau, found a place alone to sleep near the brook Jabbok.

During the night, the Bible tells us, *"Jacob, there wrestled a man with him until the breaking of the day. And when he saw that he prevailed not against him, he touched the hollow of his thigh; and the hollow of Jacob's thigh was out of joint, as he wrestled with him. And he said, Let me go, for the day breaketh. And he said, I will not let thee go, except thou bless me"* (Genesis 32:24-26).

There are several important events which occurred here.

First, Jacob was alone. God often needs to deal with us this way—without interference or influence from outside sources.

Second, he wrestles with and holds onto an angel in the form of a man. As so often happens, God uses a man to confront a man and a woman to confront a woman.

Third, Jacob hung on for dear life! The wrestling continued *"until the breaking of the day."* Jacob could have called it quits whenever he wanted. Even when the angel said, "Let go," Jacob tenaciously resisted and held tight.

Fourth, he pressed on through his pain. When the angel realized he couldn't get the best of the match, he deliberately threw Jacob's hip out of joint. He was now in great agony, yet he was still saying, "I've made a decision not to let go or give up. I won't stop until you bless my soul, my life and my situation."

As a pastor, I've seen many throw in the towel because of the pain and discomfort their present circumstances have caused.

116

They'll complain, "This battle is too hard. I'm going to quit and wait for another day."

Not Jacob. He was about to meet his brother Esau, (from whom he stole the birthright) and needed courage and help from God.

FACE TO FACE

"What is your name?" the angel asked.

"Jacob," he answered.

Then the angel announced, *"Thy name shall be called no more Jacob, but Israel: for as a prince hast thou power with God and with men, and hast prevailed"* (v.28).

All of these events took place exactly where God intended for them to happen. And Jacob named the place "Peniel"—which means "the face of God." In doing so he was saying, "I saw the Almighty face-to-face and have lived to tell the story."

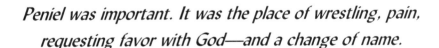

Peniel was important. It was the place of wrestling, pain, requesting favor with God—and a change of name.

Now there was birthed a *new* Jacob. His ways were transformed and God used the angel to bring blessings beyond measure. When the two brothers finally saw each other, *"Esau ran to meet him, and embraced him, and fell on his neck, and*

117

kissed him: and they wept" (Genesis 33:4).

The revelation had brought reconciliation!

Today, tell the Lord you are ready to receive His knowledge, wisdom and insight. He has shown me a clear vision for my future and He will do the same for you!

CHAPTER 13

WHAT ARE YOUR SOURCES OF INSPIRATION?

Every action of our life requires making a decision—what to cook for supper, what color of shoes to buy or where to go on vacation. Our choices, however, are often based on influence, either from the media, our friends or how we were raised.

As Christians, we must be listening to *spiritual* guidance, which come from three major sources:

1. God through the Holy Spirit.
2. Our conscience or human spirit.
3. Satan and his demons.

Being believers in Christ and a regenerated people, we need to ask ourselves these questions before responding or making a decision:

- Who is talking?
- Is this bad or good for me?
- Is this edifying to my spiritual life?
- Is it a hindrance?
- Will this give me spiritual strength?
- Will it confirm what the Lord has told me?
- Does it play on my emotions?
- Is it based on God's Word?

THE SHOWDOWN!

Influence and persuasion are powerful tools.

One of the most amazing stories in the Old Testament is the showdown on Mount Carmel between Elijah and the 450 prophets of Baal. Each side set up a sacrifice, and the god who answered by fire would be the "true" God.

The Baal worshipers tried and failed. Then it was Elijah's turn. After repairing the altar for the sacrifice, he offered this powerful prayer: *"Lord God of Abraham, Isaac, and of Israel, let it be known this day that thou art God in Israel, and that I am thy servant, and that I have done all these things at thy word. Hear me, O Lord, hear me, that this people may know that thou art the Lord God, and that thou hast turned their heart back again"* (1 Kings 18:36-37).

The fire fell and Elijah was vindicated. However, he got so carried away that he had all 450 prophets of Baal killed. Not a smart move!

King Ahab, who ruled over the land, reported to Jezebel everything Elijah had done—including the massacre. And immediately, she sent a messenger to the prophet with this threat: "The gods are going to get even with you. By this time tomorrow you will be dead just like them!"

When Elijah *"...saw that, he arose, and went for his life"* (v.3).

WHY WAS HE RUNNING?

The words he heard painted a picture in his mind of his impending death, defeat and destruction. That's why he fled.

This was the anointed prophet who had experienced miracles from God:

- The same Elijah who heard the sound of rain in the distance while putting his ear to the ground (1 Kings 18:41-16).
- The prophet who had been fed by God through ravens (1 Kings 17:6).
- The same one who was sent by the Lord to Zarephath to help a starving widow woman. She only had enough ingredients for one last cake before she and her son would die of hunger. But Elijah prophesied she was to feed *him* first. If she did, *"The barrel of meal shall not waste, neither shall the cruse of oil*

121

fail" (1 Kings 17:14). God supplied her with food until the rains came.

- This was the prophet who went into a room and stretched himself over a dead child, crying out, *"O Lord my God, I pray thee, let this child's soul come into him again"* (1 Kings 17:21). The boy was miraculously raised from the dead!

But now he was fearful and hiding from the words delivered by Jezebel. Why? The devil uses outside influences to come against what is taking place on the inside of a believer. In Elijah's case, he chose to listen to the *world!*

Weary and despondent over the negative message which had been given, the Bible records that Elijah, *"...went a day's journey into the wilderness, and came and sat down under a Juniper tree: and he requested for himself that he might die; and said, it is enough; now, O Lord, take away my life; for I am not better than my fathers"* (1 Kings 19:4).

———————❤———————

God could have left him in this depressed condition, but He wanted Elijah to get back on track and renew his mission.

So, while he was sleeping under the tree, an angel shook him and said, *"Arise and eat"* (v.5).

He looked up, *"...and, behold, there was a cake baked on the coals, and a cruse of water at his head. And he did eat and drink, and laid him down again. And the angel of the Lord came again the second time, and touched him, and said, arise and eat; because the journey is too great for thee. And he arose, and did eat and drink, and went in the strength of that meat forty nights unto Horeb the Mount of God"* (vv.6-8).

A SUPERNATURAL MEAL

Personally, I believe the angel himself prepared the food and it represents supernatural restoration for the *inside* of Elijah. After all, what earthly meal do you know of that will strengthen and satisfy you for over one month and ten days?"

Elijah was being fed the Word—which is also available to you and I today. Jesus came to *"....sanctify and cleanse it* [the church] *with the washing of water by the word"* (Ephesians 5:26). And remember, *"...man doth not live by bread only, but by every word that proceedeth out of the mouth of the Lord"* (Deuteronomy 8:3).

This is why I believe that in the food the angel prepared was the anointing, the Word and the influence of the Spirit of God.

POWERFUL INSPIRATION

Elijah arrived at Horeb—then crawled into a cave. In that place, the Word of the Lord came to him and asked, "What are you doing here?"

Elijah answered, *"I have been very jealous for the Lord God of hosts: for the children of Israel have forsaken thy covenant thrown down thine altars, and slain thy prophets with the sword; and I, even I only, am left; and they seek my life, to take it away"* (v.10).

Then he was told, *"...go forth, and stand upon the mount before the Lord. And, behold, the Lord passed by, and a great and strong wind rent the mountains, and brake in pieces the rocks before the Lord; but the Lord was not in the wind: and after the wind an earthquake; but the Lord was not in the earthquake: And after the earthquake a fire; but the Lord was not in the fire"* (vv.11-12).

God "passed by" with three dramatic manifestations: (1) a hurricane-force wind that caused the mountains to shake, (2) an earthquake and (3) a blazing fire. But the Lord was not "in" any of these.

Then, God gave Elijah the most powerful source of inspiration he ever had. Scripture tells us, *"...and after the fire a still small voice"* (v.12).

When Elijah heard this quiet voice, he muffled his face with his cloak and stood in the mouth of the cave. Once more, he was asked, "What are you doing here, Elijah?

In that moment, God gave the prophet clear directions regarding where he was to go—and where to find a remnant of believers who had not bowed down to Baal. It was on this journey, Elijah met a young man plowing in a field. His name was Elisha—who followed the prophet at God's leading and

124

became his right-hand man (vv.19-21).

"DON'T LOOK AT THE STORM"

The still small voice is symbolic of the Holy Spirit who works within every born again believer. It is our true source of inspiration and influence.

———————♥———————

Regardless of what is taking place around us,
the familiar voice of God is gently speaking inside.

He is reminding us, "Do not look at the storm, the earthquake or the fire. Ignore the devil's threats, your circumstances and the negative conversations of unbelievers. I will speak quietly to you through the Holy Spirit."

For forty days Elijah was cowering in fear and out of the will of God. He allowed Satan to use the "external" to bind up the "internal"—where the Lord speaks.

When the truth was finally revealed, the Lord let Elijah know that He had not changed His mind—and that he was still a prophet.

THE SPIRIT'S DIRECTION

In the words of Jesus, *"...when he, the Spirit of Truth, is come, he will guide you into all truth"* (John 13:13). The Greek word for *guide* is "kateuthuno," meaning to direct or lead.

The verse continues, *"...for he shall not speak of himself, but whatsoever he shall hear, that shall he speak, and he will show you things to come"* (v.13). The word *show* is "photeinos," which is to make transparent. God gives light to our soul and makes Christ real to our innermost being.

Then Jesus explains, *"He shall glorify me: for he shall receive of mine and shall show it unto you. All things that the Father hath are mine: therefore said I that he shall take of mine, and shall show it unto you"* (vv.14-15).

Christ is speaking in the first person. The Holy Spirit and His ministry of direction, instruction and influence in the life of the believer is representing Jesus on earth.

The Spirit of God will help us communicate and fellowship with Christ and the Father. He will help us understand a revelation and offers deeper truth and greater insight.

The epistles were written under His guidance. Paul and the remaining apostles wrote through the persuasion and direction of the Holy Spirit.

KEPT BY THE WORD

The inspiration of the Word is powerful in both the Old and New Testaments.

One day I read these words in the book of Judges concerning the children of Israel. *"And they were to prove Israel by them, to know whether they would hearken unto the commandments of the Lord, which he commended their fathers by the hand of Moses. And the children of Israel dwelt among the Canaanites, Hittites, and Amorites, and Perizzites, and Hivites and Jebusites: And they took their daughters to be their wives, and gave their daughters to their sons, and served their gods"* (Judges 3:4-6).

God left these nations alone, to see if Israel would continue to live as *His* people and not allow these cultures to persuade them.

As I was studying scripture, I asked the Lord to reveal to me why He didn't *remove* them from carnal influences so the children of Israel wouldn't be tempted or swayed to go astray. The Spirit led me to read the words of Jesus in John's gospel: *"I have given them thy word; and the world hath hated them, because they are not of the world, even as I am not of the world. I pray not that thou shouldest take them out of the world, but that thou shouldest keep them from the evil"* (John 17:15).

The key words are: *"I have given them thy word."* God's people are to be directed and kept *only* by the Word.

Israel failed because they allowed themselves to be affected by what was going on around them. They took on the lifestyles, habits, ideas and even the "gods" of these evil nations.

Oh, if people would only live according to the words of the prophet Isaiah: *"Thou wilt keep him in perfect peace, whose mind is stayed on thee: because he trusteth in thee"* (Isaiah 26:3).

STAY FOCUSED

James Allen, author of *As A Man Thinketh*, notes, "Today we are where our thoughts have taken us, and that we are the architects—for better or worse—of our future."

Is it your desire to keep your mind focused on Christ? Remember:

1. God wants us to hear His voice—inwardly.
2. He desires for us to learn to respond properly and timely to His leading.
3. Listen and listen again to His voice by establishing and training yourself to recognize when He is speaking to you.
4. Be in continuous communion with Him through the Word, prayer and fasting.

Satan works at a feverish pitch to keep God's voice from being clearly heard and recognized by the believer. He floods and "jams" our minds with outside attacks including fear, frustrations and doubt. Then he blocks our faith regarding spiritual matters by drawing us to what we can see, feel, taste, smell, and hear—the physical realm of our resources.

THE "EXTERNAL" FACTORS

What Satan did to the thoughts of Judas should be a warning. The Bible records, *"And supper being ended, the devil having now put into the heart of Judas Iscariot, Simon's son, to betray him"* (John 13:2).

The devil came from the *outside*—infiltrating the mind and heart of Judas, manipulating his feelings, causing him to make the decision to betray Jesus.

———————❤———————

Satan will always use external factors
because he and the Holy Ghost cannot reside
in the believer at the same time.

So while the Spirit works inwardly revealing God's will and plan to us, Satan works outwardly with circumstances to come against us.

If you want to know the extent of the devil's influence, read the story of Ananias and Sapphira (Acts 5:1-10). Yet, there is a way to defeat the enemy. Study Jesus' personal encounter with Satan (Matthew 4:1-11) and you'll learn how to wield the power of the Word.

What is your source of inspiration? Who is having the greatest impact on you? Satan or the Savior?

It's been said, "Birds of a feather flock together." Be careful who you are associating with—and who you are listening to.

CHAPTER 14

THE SIX PHASES OF WAITING ON THE LORD

T he most demanding, and often frustrating, activity of God's people is waiting patiently for an answer from the Lord.

We are always in a hurry and think the Almighty should give us a response as fast as the click of the mouse on our computer. But God communicates with His people in a totally different manner. As believers, the answers we so desperately search for come in a variety of ways—through dreams, visions, promptings and convictions of the Holy Spirit as well as the written and spoken Word of God.

The Lord will reveal His answers to us, *"...by his Spirit: for the Spirit searcheth all things, yea, the deep things of God"* (1 Corinthians 2:10). And during those times when we don't even know what to pray for, *"...the Spirit itself maketh intercession for us with groanings which cannot be uttered"* (Romans 8:26).

Receiving and experiencing all of the Father's plans depends on our waiting, persevering and maintaining our place in Him—knowing we are anticipating from God what He has told us to expect from Him and His Word.

Although we face many challenges, God is worthy to be trusted and is always faithful as He has promised. Waiting on the Lord teaches us that everything in His will happens according to His predestinated schedule.

By understanding this, we rid ourselves of every nagging and disturbing emotion which attacks and "rattles" our ability to seek and receive the fulfillment of God's Word.

Let me shares six phases of waiting on the Lord:

PHASE I

ANTICIPATION

One of the most valuable inner virtues God has placed in our minds and hearts is the ability to anticipate or expect. It is not something we can conjure up by ourselves. As the psalmist writes, *"My soul, wait thou only upon God; for my expectation is from him"* (Psalm 62:5).

Positive anticipation is a foundation stone and key functioning element of our faith and belief. We consider what God has promised as certain and this allows us to see how He obligates Himself to fulfill what He has said to us—thus deepening our commitment to depend on Him.

Remember, on God's calendar, *"...there is a season, and a*

time to every purpose under the heaven" (Ecclesiastes 3:1). And *"He hath made everything beautiful in his time"* (v.11).

So important is our personal ability to hold onto this Word, which is literally Him. *"In the beginning was the Word, and the Word was with God, and the Word was God"* (John 1:1).

Through the writers of the Holy Scriptures, God Himself is actually painting a picture of His actions in "operational phases"—stage after stage, condition after condition, need after need.

———————💗———————

In advance, the Lord reassures us that no matter what the trial or test we face, it will not keep us from ultimate victory.

Why? Because He has already given us His Word that all we have to do is believe for the answer.

Hang in there! Expect and anticipate His promises.

When you are confronted with Satan's schemes, totally ignore them. The devil attempts to make you give up and give in to every pressure of life. He is whispering in your ear, "Surrender! Relinquish your hope. Go ahead and admit defeat and failure because they are waiting just around the corner."

He even tries to have you focus on your greatest need—just so you will question God's faithfulness to you.

These elements of pressure and manipulation from Satan will

begin to take root in a person who is:

1. Insecure in knowing the dependability of God.
2. Unable to locate in God's Word where the promise for a specific need is written.
3. Possessing no previous experience of the Lord bringing victory after waiting and resting in His promises.

Never give up on God. Learn to remain steadfast where you are *spiritually* and hold onto what you have already gained and achieved up to this point. Look for examples of fellow Christians around you and feed on their testimonies of God's faithfulness to them. Turn to scripture and read of the people to whom He fulfilled His Word.

Use the sword of the spirit (Ephesians 6) which is the Word of God—His written weapon.

Stay in your assigned place with Him—remaining in readiness and expectation until the answer arrives.

.

PHASE 2

TRUST

The pattern of relying on God and building trust in Him comes from repeatedly hearing the Father's promises to us— over and over again. Because each time there comes a different pressure and attack on the mind and emotions. This is reinforced as we witness and hear of men and women who persistently waited on the Lord and He met their need.

Such people live with this assurance: *"Commit thy way unto the Lord; trust also in him; and he shall bring it to pass"* (Psalm 37:5). "Faith cometh..." (Romans 10:17)—which means the pattern of trusting God and *receiving* that trust comes from hearing His promises to us over and over and over again!

The Word of God encourages us, *"Be ye followers of them who through faith and patience inherit the promises of God"* (Hebrews 6:12). Imitate them and pattern yourself after their example. Study what they demonstrate in their Christian walk and put these same practices into action.

In the above scripture, we are told to be followers of *"them"*—which means not everybody *did* or not everybody *will* inherit the promises.

It's easy to grow weary and give up, so you must focus on strong-minded people who found a way to *persevere*, to hold fast and press on. They received the blessing from waiting on God.

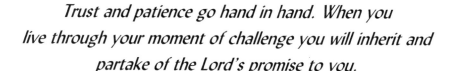

Trust and patience go hand in hand. When you live through your moment of challenge you will inherit and partake of the Lord's promise to you.

You can't trust God's Word only on Sunday and doubt Him

on Monday. The Bible says, *A double-minded man is unstable in all his ways"* (James 1:8). He is *"...like a wave of the sea driven with the wind and tossed"* (v.6).

What happens to a person who tries to sit on both sides of the fence—the spiritual side and the carnal? Of the double minded person, the scripture concludes, *"... let not that man think that he shall receive anything from the Lord"* (v.8).

PHASE 3

FAITH

We must, by faith, believe, seek and trust Him for His existence as God—and that He never changes from His eternal position. Faith is the main ingredient of waiting.

As the Word tells us, *"But without faith it is impossible to please Him: for he that cometh to God must believe that he is, and that he is a rewarder of them that diligently seek him"* (Hebrews 11:6).

Our faith pays awesome dividends. The Lord is a generous giver who responds with favor and blessing when we approach Him.

Throughout my journey of 30-plus years with Christ, I have had to continually wait, expect and watch for Him—always ready to receive His favor. At the same time I have learned to resist and rebuke the devil, renouncing every negative word he places in my mind.

The Lord has declared this sacred vow: *"...before they call,*

I will answer; and while they are yet speaking, I will hear" (Isaiah 65:24). This promise was first made to the nation of Israel at a critical moment in their destiny—and it is for us today.

Faith is the anchor which holds firm and allows you to wait on God, whether the answer comes immediately, next week or in the future. The Lord, however, talks about faith in the present tense: *"Now faith is "the substance of things hoped for, the evidence of things not seen"* (Hebrews 11:1).

Do you have "now" faith so you will be able to receive the reality?

PHASE 4

WORK

I've met those who make their request known to the Lord, then sit in a corner and just wait. Friend, that's not the way it happens. God expects you to be active—about your Father's business. Jesus says, *"Occupy till I come"* (Luke 19:13).

"Waiting" is not standing idly by, doing nothing and going nowhere. Instead it is a time of personal growth as you face challenge after challenge—continuously seeing God ahead of you and trusting Him for the manifestation. You are moving forward with assurance that the Lord will fulfill what He has promised. In the process, you know in your heart of hearts that your waiting will not be in vain.

Keep working in God's vineyard. What the Lord has done

for others, He will surely do for you. As scripture tells us, *"For whatsoever things were written aforetime were written for our learning, that we through patience and comfort of the scriptures might have hope"* (Romans 15:4).

———————❤———————

God has prepared His written Word to teach us how those in another generations served the Lord just as we do. They depended on the Almighty for their protection, preservation, maintenance and fulfillment of His plan in their lives.

Did some fall by the wayside? Certainly. But thank God for those who kept the faith, standing against insurmountable odds.

Think of God's pre-planning. Before we would arrive at any trial or need, He prepared a "witness" or "expert" reporter, who lived the story and saved for us the record of an unchanging God and His faithfulness. It was to educate us by showing us the example of early saints.

This was all accomplished to provide for us undeniable proof that all of these things, item by item, have been written and stamped with God's witness of trustworthiness.

This *authorizes* and *empowers* faith in *us*—removing all uncertainty. You see, doubt activates suspicion, which causes alarm and panic. As a result we can become misdirected and make decisions outside of God's will.

When we fail to wait on the Lord to fulfill His plan, we are tempted to alter our course by inserting our own objectives— and eclipsing God's. When this happens, the end result brings shipwreck, fragmented destiny and *unfinished assignments,* producing early and premature fruit that withers away; never fulfilling our purpose.

When the Lord gives you a vision, start working—and don't stop until it becomes a reality

PHASE 5
TESTING

While you are waiting, your faith is being tried to perfection. As such, waiting on the Lord is not a bed of roses or a stroll down Easy Street. Scripture declares, *"...the trying of your faith worketh patience"* (James 1:3).

The word trying ("dokimion" in Greek) denotes a testing or trial of trustworthiness.

As you probably know, a courtroom trial is a time of inquiry, searching and researching followed by both an examination and an intense *cross*-examination. The goal is to know that the ultimate decision is beyond question or dispute.

In the Christian life our faith is also tried—both by the world and by God Himself. Are you totally convinced what God has said is true? Are you certain He has performed what He claims? Are His works evident today?

Let me share a verse which has given me confidence in the Almighty and a strong spiritual "footing" in my walk with Him. The psalmist writes, *"As for God, his way is perfect: the word of the Lord is tried..."* (Psalm 18:30).

God who is the Owner and Master over all, is flawless—and so are the methods He chooses and uses to bring manifestations of His perfect will. Nothing needs to be added or subtracted. Yet, while it is happening, He permits His Word and His decisions to be tested. So you see, it is God's Word *to* us, *about* us and *for* us which is on trial *in* us.

This is a powerful principle.

———————❤———————

The trials and tests you face are not directed at you alone, but toward God <u>in you</u>!

In order for us to experience fulfillment, the Almighty permits His infallible Word to be confronted by Satan, physical pain, emotional strain, financial demands and personal situations. When these problems arise, we must respond with what the Word tells us: *"But my God shall supply all your need according to his riches in glory by Christ Jesus"* (Philippians 4:19).

The psalmist explains this even further by saying, *"The words of the Lord are pure words: as silver tried in a furnace of earth, purified seven times"* (Psalms 12:6). I love the Hebrew meaning of *tried*—"tsaraph"—to refine like a goldsmith who uses fire to purge away the impurities and useless materials in gold or silver. He separates the dross from the molded and sharpened vessel.

By comparison, in us, the part that must be separated is our natural suspicions and calculating thoughts which shake our trust in God and make us want to run away rather than to stand still and wait on Him.

Remember, until the Lord is ready to move on our behalf, we must rely totally on God to bring to reality His spoken Word in our lives. He decides the plan, puts it into action and uses His power to bring it to pass. Our job is to simply believe God and withstand every arrow which comes against us.

We will only be able to accomplish this with faith that has been tested and proven to be what we spoke of earlier: the *"substance of things hoped for and evidence of things not seen"* (Hebrews 11:1).

Waiting is never easy—it is one of the most difficult times in a believer's existence. The only way to survive is to have the guaranteed support of the Word. Thank God, *"...the testimony of the Lord is sure"* (Psalm 19:7).

The meaning of "testimony" is to have the Father's personal report of His works written in the Bible. To identify the people who have waited and seen God come through in their lives is our greatest strength.

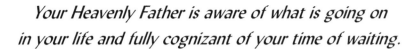

*Your Heavenly Father is aware of what is going on
in your life and fully cognizant of your time of waiting.*

More important, however, is the fact He has mapped out a path to take you from where you are to the destiny He has planned. Your resources will manifest themselves. The answer *will* come and you will be *rewarded*, not disappointed.

While you patiently wait, stay in constant communication with God through prayer—allowing Him to speak to your heart and spirit. Through every trial, the Lord will reassure and comfort His children. He knows that during this period of anticipation and expectation you need fellowship with Him.

PHASE 6

ENDURANCE

Waiting is all about abiding and enduring in your circumstances until the Lord's appointed time. Yes, there is a designated schedule for all things which God established before the foundation of the world. Everything that transpires was predetermined and cannot—and *will* not— take place before He gives the signal.

When that moment arrives, it seems there is a "domino" effect of events which are triggered—and blessings upon blessings follow in our lives. Other events are set off because of this.

142

In the meantime, believing God for the manifestation strengthens our spirit, deepens our resolve and intensifies our faith. Confidence in God is often our only support—yet He is all we ever need. His proven record, the Word of God, gives us the endurance we require.

We are sustained by the fact our God has never lied and *cannot* lie.

On our journey here on earth, the Father may send what I call "faith-testers" to determine our level of self-abandonment and confidence in Him. At the same time, the devil will send "fear-givers" to test our patience and love for God. Satan plans to interfere and eliminate any further manifestations and greater spiritual levels from being reached.

During this difficult period, the path may have many twists and turns and we will be confronted by surprises. Yet God, in His endless wisdom, has searched out and predetermined every step we take. To us, however, it may seem like a confusing maze.

———————❤———————

The fuel which makes continuing
possible is our previous achievements,
blessings and the past promises
we have obtained from the Lord.

It's so easy to weaken and say, "This is as far as I can

possibly go," but remember it was *"the joy that was set before him"* (Hebrew 12:2) that allowed Jesus to endure the cross.

Let that same joy of the future rekindle your faith.

Sometimes, different thoughts, emotions and suspicions take place in our hearts and there are replays of what has already been achieved.

If you are torn between the victories of the past and the apprehensions of the unseen, put your faith in God's character—which is from everlasting to everlasting.

Look up to heaven and say, *"Thou art my God"* (Psalm 31:14). You serve the Almighty who declares, *"...I am the Lord, I change not"* (Malachi 3:6).

As the self-sustaining creator of all things, He is immutable, unchanging and the God who remains forever. He is our Redeemer, Deliverer, Defender, Healer and Provider. His wisdom is eternal.

How then can a God who is "forever who He is," fail to reward one who is waiting on His Word?

What a contrast from Satan's character—a liar, deceiver, destroyer, and hater of God's people, God's power and even God Himself.

Envy and jealousy rule the devil. Revenge drives him and his demons —angels who chose to commit themselves to his failed mission of trying to be like God.

———————❤———————

Satan is no match for the One who created him.
How can he possibly outsmart God, whose wisdom
thought up every phase of his being, his
imagination and his decision making?

God never allows anything to exceed Him. The one who creates never places all of His own ability and potential into His creation.

All of Satan's life is derived totally from God's design. As scripture states, *"All things were made by him; and without him was not any thing made that was made"* (John 1:3).

You may ask, "If God created him, why does the devil do such horrible things?"

The answer is the same for Satan as it is for us: we have been given a free will and can choose to accept or reject God's will.

One thing is certain; Satan and his demons cannot outsmart or out-maneuver us as long as God is leading. Our guarantee is God's character, which never changes.

Waiting, then, is a gift from God. It was made and designed by Him before time itself—pre-assigned into every person in the body of Christ.

We also know: *"...he that shall endure unto the end, the same shall be saved"* (Mark 13:13).

Diligently obeying God's Word equips and gives us the endurance necessary to travel through the deepest valley. The

Word is the only support system we need until the day when the Father's will is revealed to us—and, thank God, that day is written on His calendar!

The capacity of waiting is a gift of the Father given to us. Before the time we need to use it, the gift was foreseen and pre-assigned to you by God.

CHAPTER 15

VELVET TONGUES WITH CLOTHES THAT MATCH

Communication has only one goal: to give clear and precise directions which will cause the recipient to receive and react in the manner the communiqué is intended.

For example, the reason for advertising and marketing is to present an event, product, person, place, service or benefit available to a vast number of people. A department store may promote designer suits—but they are mass produced in multiple sizes, colors and designs.

"Velvet tongues" is a phrase used to describe those who can successfully—and smoothly—verbalize their dreams and goals to the point that others are ready to join their efforts. This is in contrast to a person who uses condescension, hyperbole or even mockery to sell their idea. That style may attract attention, yet it rarely works.

As you will see, it's not just what you think or say that is important, but do you have the lifestyle which demonstrates and exemplifies your words?

YOUR STOREHOUSE

Jesus declares, *"...for out of the abundance* [overflow, plenty] *of the heart the mouth speaketh"* (Matthew 12:13).

———————♥———————

You have a storehouse within—the sum total
of what possesses your mind, will and emotions.

It is the reservoir from which we excel in life. And when you are so filled with blessings and favor, you can't help but share them outwardly in your conversations with others.

What you are consumed with ignites your thoughts, desires and your vocabulary.

ELOQUENT WORDS

Internal achievement is about seeing your inward, invisible, accomplishments first then outwardly experiencing them. The wisdom we attain academically, financially, physically or spiritually must take place mentally. The blueprint for action begins there. Then you are ready for the verbal expression and visible experience to take place. "I see it. I mentally design it and I physically wear it"—velvet tongues with clothes that match!

As recorded in scripture, God uses Moses to describe the destiny of Joseph in eloquent, graceful words: *"And of Joseph he said blessed of the Lord be his land for the precious things of heaven, for the dew, and for the deep that coucheth beneath. And for the precious fruits brought forth by the sun, and for the precious things put forth by the moon. For the chief things of the ancient mountains, and for the precious things of the lasting hills. And for the precious things of the earth and fullness thereof, and for the good will of him that dwelt in the bush; let the blessing come upon the head of Joseph and upon the top of the head of him that was separated from his brethren. His glory is like the firstling of his bullock, and his thorns are like the horns of unicorns; with them he shall push the people together to the ends of the earth; and they are the ten thousand of Ephraim and they are thousands of Manasseh"* (Deuteronomy 33:13-17).

Much earlier, in Genesis 37-50, we see how Joseph went through every stage of this poetic description—internally, mentally, emotionally and physically. This "dreamer," who was sold into slavery by his own brothers, emerged in Egypt and rose to such a place of leadership that he was called Zaphnathpaaneah by Pharaoh (Genesis 41:44). This name means "preserver of life, savior of the world, the bread of life."

NEW GARMENTS

What an historic day it was when Pharoah *"took off his ring from his hand, and put it upon Joseph's hand, and arrayed him in vestures of fine linen, and put a gold chain about his neck...and he made him ruler over all the land of Egypt"* (vv.42-43). The people bowed before him.

The image of God's eventual elevation lived inside Joseph for 13 years. From the pit, to the prison, to the palace. God was with him, developing every detail of the velvet words which expressed who he was in the plan of God, and what he would ultimately experience.

Secular writers have used a unicorn to describe Joseph. It is a mythical creature resembling a horse with a single horn in the center of its forehead; which is often a symbol of chastity or purity.

Joseph's experiences were unimaginable, yet his character remained untainted. Nothing he did rendered him to be unfit to become what God showed Joseph in the dream.

Our velvet words, when they are clothed in the purity of our heart, become our cover and protection from failure. They keep us focused through whatever we encounter and lead us to the place of honor the Lord is preparing.

CHAPTER 16

FOOTSTEPS ON THE INSIDE

B ehind every success in life there is an invisible path that is mentally traveled—a road which has been walked over and over again in your thoughts.

Every step we take starts with an image or a concept, and even our starting and stopping first takes place in our mind. This determines the difference between:

- Hesitation or motivation.
- Procrastination or demonstration.
- Failure or achievement.

Where and how we walk, however, depends on our purpose, goals and intentions—and the time available to complete the task.

The great turning points in the history of God's people were the direct result of divine instructions penetrating the heart of a dedicated servant. Let me share these examples:

"ARISE! WALK THROUGH THE LAND!"

In the early days of Abram (before his name was changed to Abraham) God did more than "call" him by voice. The Almighty painted a visual picture in his mind of what was about to take place.

The Lord said Abram, *"... lift up not thine eyes, and look from the place where thou art northward, and southward, and eastward, and westward: For all the land which thou seest, to thee will I give it, and thy seed forever"* (Genesis 13:14-15).

Then God gave Abram this important directive: *"Arise, walk through the land in the length of it and in the breadth of it; for I will give it unto thee"* (v.17).

———————— ♥ ————————

Before the Lord asked Abraham to physically take footsteps on the outside, He inspired the "Father of Nations" to mentally take footsteps on the inside.

HE ENVISIONED THE RESULTS

Many years later, after both Abraham and Moses had left this earth, God spoke these words to Joshua, the newly appointed leader of the children of Israel: *"Every place that the sole of your foot shall tread upon, that have I given unto you, as I said unto Moses. From the wilderness and this Lebanon even unto the great river, the river Euphrates, all the land of the Hittites, and unto the great sea toward the going down of the sun, shall be your coast"* (Joshua 1:3-4).

That's over 300,000 square miles!

Joshua was 80 years old when his assignment was first etched within him. Then, as the Lord spoke, he envisioned the results.

Before "the sole of his foot" trod the land, he saw footsteps on the inside which caused him to walk toward his destiny. During the next 20-plus years of leadership, Joshua *"...took all that land, the hills, and all the south country, and all the land of Goshen, and the valley, and the plain, and the mountain of Israel, and the valley of the same* (Joshua 11:16). And he *...gave it for an inheritance unto Israel"* (v.23).

BEFORE THE TRUMPETS BLEW

In Sunday School we sang about Joshua at the battle of Jericho and how the walls came tumbling down.

In the story, however, we find a man of God who saw victory in his mind's eye long before the trumpets blew and the army marched around the city.

The Bible tells us, *"And the Lord said unto Joshua, See [inwardly] I have given into thy hands Jericho, and the king thereof, and the mighty men of valor. And ye shall compass the city, all ye men of war, and go round aobut the city once, thus shalt thou do six days. And seven priests shall bear before the ark seven trumpets of rams' horns: and the seventh day ye shall compass the city seven times, and the priests shall blow with the trumpets"* (Joshua 6:2-4).

The Lord is giving strategic instructions to Joshua to relay to the people. Each of them has to first mentally and internally "walk out" the directions in their thoughts—then physically demonstrate what they practiced in their minds.

Here was the result. Scripture records, *"...it came to pass, when the people heard the sound of the trumpet, and the people shouted with a great shout, that the wall fell down flat, so that the people went up...and they took the city"* (v.20).

Victory came because every man and women under Joshua's command completely obeyed the vision God had released.

SEE YOURSELF AS A CONQUEROR

Throughout his years of leadership the Lord painted picture after picture in the heart of Joshua.

———— ♥ ————

He could visualize successfully removing military threats so the children of Israel could survive in Canaan.

He saw his people victorious in a five-year war against 31 different kings (Joshua 12). God showed him the precise boundaries and cities for all the tribes of Israel (Joshua 13).

Even at the age of 100, God told him, *"...there remaineth yet very much land to be possessed"* (Joshua 13:1).

Every victory was a vindication of what the Lord had already shown him. For example, even before Joshua's troops marched on Ai, God declared, *"Fear not...I have given into thy hand the king of Ai, and his people, and his city, and his land"* (Joshua 8:1).

Friend, we go nowhere and accomplish nothing until we first see ourselves as conquerors—whether the battle is financial, relational or spiritual.

IT WILL HAPPEN FOR YOU!

As you have read this book, you may have thought, "This is the kind of life I want to live."

It will never happen until you make a personal commitment to continually feed your mind with the promises of the Father.

- Read God's Word and commit key verses to memory.
- Day after day, stake your claim based on your covenant with Him.
- Visualize the Lord helping you in every situation.
- Dream big dreams.
- See yourself accomplishing challenging goals and objectives.

When God gives you a purpose He will also give you the provision to make it a reality. The footsteps on the inside are not the product of your imagination. They are placed there by the Lord Himself, and He expects you to follow them all the days of your life.

I am praying that your internal achievement will bring honor to the Lord, joy to your life and touch the world for Christ.

NOTES

FOR A COMPLETE LIST OF RESOURCES
OR TO SCHEDULE THE AUTHOR FOR
SPEAKING ENGAGEMENTS,
CONTACT:

WALTER LEIGH BATES
BALM IN GILEAD FOR ALL PEOPLE INTERNATIONAL
1210 S. 61ST STREET
WEST ALLIS, WI 53214

PHONE 414-228-7344